Pat & Chas —
for your enlightenment as to
what Findhorn is all about
'75
Emile &
Suzannah

The Findhorn Garden

One radiant energy pervades and gives rise to all life. While it may speak to us through plants, nature spirits or the human beings with whom we share life on this planet, all are reflections of the deeper reality behind and within them. Myth has become reality in the Findhorn garden, not to present us with a new form of spiritualism, but to offer us a new vision of life, a vision of unity. Essentially, the devas and nature spirits are aspects of our own selves, guiding us toward our true identity, the divine reality within. The story of the garden is the celebration of this divine life in its myriad forms. May the joy we experience in participating in this celebration deepen our commitment to revealing the total beauty of ourselves and all life around us.

This volume is part of a series of books to be published by Harper & Row, Publishers, Inc., for the Lindisfarne Association. The series is under the general editorship of William Irwin Thompson and will be devoted to an exploration of the newly emerging planetary society and the future evolution of man.

Other books in the Lindisfarne series

PASSAGES ABOUT EARTH: An Exploration of the New Planetary Culture
by William Irwin Thompson

SRI AUROBINDO, OR THE ADVENTURE OF CONSCIOUSNESS
by Satprem

THE FINDHORN GARDEN

by The Findhorn Community

Foreword by William Irwin Thompson

Harper & Row, Publishers
New York, Evanston, San Francisco, London

Some portions of this book are adapted from *The Findhorn Garden: An Experiment in the Co-Operation Between Three Kingdoms* booklets, which were first printed and published by The Findhorn Trust in 1968.

FIRST EDITION

LIBRARY OF CONGRESS CATALOG NUMBER: 75-6335

ISBN: 0-06-011249-2 (cloth)

ISBN: 0-06-011251-4 (paper)

Compiling and Editing: Shoshana Tembeck
Editorial and Business Advisor: Kevin Curley
Layout and Design: Frank Stong
Photography: Kathy Thormod and Will Elwell
Typography: Mary Stanton, Dobrinka Popov and Sono Enseki

THE FINDHORN GARDEN book is an expression of the love and energy of the entire Findhorn family. Except for the final printing, all aspects of the work have taken place within the community. This has given many of us the opportunity to participate directly in the alchemy of the creative process. Through it we have experienced the challenges and joys that have led to our transformation.

While we would wish to thank many individually for their contributions, here we can only mention a few. Without question, our first thanks goes to those who began Findhorn's cooperation with the nature kingdoms: Peter and Eileen Caddy, Dorothy Maclean, the late R. Ogilvie Crombie, and David Spangler whose presence led Findhorn beyond the garden and into the community that it is today. Paul Hawken initially developed the vision for the revised edition of the original Findhorn Garden booklets. His support and understanding, as well as that of Rachel Friedlander and Chris Connolly, helped establish the work in its beginning stages.

Hours of lectures, interviews and discussions were transcribed by Ann Barton, Karen Hogg, and especially Sara Mariott and Sono. From this material, as well as personal writings, the chapters on Peter, Eileen and Dorothy were developed. Expressed in their own words, these chapters seek to convey not only the story and essence of Findhorn but also the character and energy of these individuals.

Rather than restricting ourselves to individual tasks, each of us has contributed in some way to every aspect of the book. Besides Kevin's invaluable editorial work, others in the community who have been of particular help in drawing the text together are Lida Sims, John Hilton, Jennifer Murray, Ian Campbell, Andrew Murray and Roy McVicar. The patience, dedication and aesthetic sensibility of those involved in typesetting have played a major part in fulfilling the standard of perfection toward which we work.

In the final chapter, Lida has reflected the thoughts and feelings of the Findhorn gardeners, past and present, in answer to questions on our practical gardening techniques and on our understanding of the nature of cooperation. Tom Earle has contributed the description of the garden and its main work program. The answer to the question on compost is based on a lecture given in the community by Holger Welz. The quotes on pages 160 and 162 are from Fred Barton, Michael Bucke, Holger and Sona. The sequel and the thoughts expressed in answer to the question on practical oneness have been contributed by Shoshana.

In addition to the many hours that Kathy and Will have spent shooting, printing and selecting photographs, others have also contributed: Jim Bronson, Arthur Bailey, Crispin Current, Robyn Gormley, Frances Ross-Smith, Paul Plagerson and David Clapham. David has also made all the photostatic prints needed for the final format and design. The photographs of children in Eileen's chapter have been contributed by Georgia Longini. Under Frank's direction, David Nez, Irena Majcen and Isa Petrikat have assembled text and photos for the finished art mechanicals. Mary Inglis and the publications department have given us their space, warmth and support.

Many others from outside the community have also given their assistance. We would particularly like to express our appreciation to Buz Wyeth and Lynne McNabb at Harper & Row for their trust, encouragement and friendship.

In thanksgiving to these individuals and to all the forms of divine energy that have brought this book and Findhorn into being, we wish to dedicate THE FINDHORN GARDEN to the Earth which has given birth to us all.

CONTENTS

FOREWORD. No two places could be less alike than Findhorn and the Stanford Research Institute. SRI is one of the largest think tank contractors for the Department of Defense and receives over sixty million dollars a year from government, industry and foundations. Findhorn is a small spiritual community in the north of Scotland which is funded by faith that God will meet its needs if the community follows the esoteric "laws of manifestation." At SRI they talk to the important people of the world, but at Findhorn they talk to the plants in the garden. And the plants seem to like it so much that they respond by growing out of sand and blossoming in the snow. The miraculous garden of men and plants has become modestly famous, and in the last few years three different books have focused on the way of life there. It is time that the community of man and plants spoke for themselves, and thus this book appears, written, photographed and designed by the members of Findhorn. But to appreciate the book within the context of contemporary global culture, one should read it alongside the Stanford Research Institute's recent monograph, *Changing Images of Man.*

Changing Images of Man is Policy Report 4 of SRI's Center for the Study of Social Policy. It is ironic to see a think tank calling for the creation of a new image of man in a new culture and then producing an American behavioral science monograph that is part and parcel of the old world view. But it is even more amusing to realize that the people who would nod in affirmation at SRI's conclusions are the very ones who would be repelled by Findhorn. Nevertheless, the fact is that what is being talked about at SRI is being done at Findhorn.

> Now questions of tremendous import arise. Could an image of humankind emerge that might shape the future, as the currently dominant images—man as the master of nature, inhabitant of a material world, and consumer of goods—our legacy of the past, have shaped our present culture? Could such a new image provide the bridge to carry us safely over to a post-industrial era? If so, what characteristics should the emergent image entail, such that it would be both feasible and adequate for the satisfactory resolution of the serious problems currently facing the society?
>
> From the nature of contemporary societal problems, studies of plausible alternative futures, and our earlier considerations of the role played by a society's dominant image, we can postulate a provisional list of characteristics that a new image must possess if it is to become dominant and effective. At the minimum we believe it would need to: (1) provide a holistic sense of perspective on life, (2) entail an ecological ethic, (3) entail a self-realization ethic, (4) be multi-leveled, multi-faceted and integrative, (5) lead to a balancing and coordinating of satisfactions along many dimensions, and (6) be experimental and open-ended.[1]

It all sounds well and good, but to those more familiar with the world of the behavioral sciences the monograph is really talking about the attempt of American social science (or what the report calls, with delusions of grandeur, "the policy sciences") to absorb culture into new forms of administrative control or cultural management. To do this effectively, Management must understand how culture works, how myths are generated, and how new images of man are created; therefore, hitherto alien areas like religion and the humanities must be absorbed and pushed through the flow charts of systems theory. Although the report calls for a shift away from the image of man in which the individual is separate from nature, every line of the volume reveals the very mentality it is trying to escape. American social science, from the victory of the United States in 1945 to the victory of the North Vietnamese in 1975, tried to "develop" the world by replacing traditional cultures with behavioral science ideologies of "modernization." The leaders of this movement were star-gazers in the courts of the imperial Presidents, savants like Walt Rostow and McGeorge Bundy. With the fall of Saigon and the failure of the Green Revolution, it is obvious that the historical limits to modernization have been reached; nevertheless, Policy Report 4 goes bravely on in the path of modernization as it struggles to replace the atavisms of religion and the humanities with "the policy sciences."

> Thus science [in parapsychological research] has legitimated systematic exploration of those realms of human experience in which our deepest value commitments have their source and which had hitherto been left to religion and the humanities.[2]

To produce this report, the Center for the Study of Social Policy received a quarter of a million dollars from the Charles F. Kettering Foundation. They received the grant because the world of post-industrial society is an interlocking directorate of the corporate systems of government, foundations, universities and industry. American social science is expensive, but any traditional historian could have told the social scientists and the foundation executives for a song that culture simply does not work the way "the policy sciences" think. New images of man do not spring from Policy Research Reports; all cultures begin in explosions of myth in the minds of prophets, mystics, visionary scientists, artists and crazies. Whether it is in the dreams of Descartes, Alfred Russell Wallace and Niels Bohr, or in the visions of Buddha, Jesus and Mohammed, culture springs from the depths no behavioral science can touch and still remain behavioral. The distance from prophecy to professorship is great, but even the founders of social science were much crazier than their contemporary routine followers, for Marx, Comte, Durkheim, Spencer, Saint Simon and Fourier were rather visionary in their sweep of ideas. It is, therefore, highly amusing to think that the administrators in the Kettering Foundation who granted SRI the quarter of a million would be horrified by the book now in your hands and could not see that the new world view and the new image of man are already embodied, not in a report, but in the living culture of the community of Findhorn.

Those who are likely to respond to *The Findhorn Garden* are those who can set it on the shelf alongside their copies of *The Book of the Hopi, The Tibetan Book of the Dead,* and *Journey to Ixtlan.* Now that we have taken in the visions of Hopi, Tibetan, and Yaqui cultures, it is time for us to welcome the stranger in our own Western tradition. From the esoteric point of view, of course, there is only one tradition. Whether we speak of kachinas, devas, djin, angels or sprites, we are invoking a cosmology that is much the same around the world.

Industrialization tried to drive that cosmology out of men's minds, but now that the failure of the

Green Revolution has dramatized the failure of the industrialization of agriculture, the underground traditions of animism can surface without any sense of embarrassment. It is the proponents of the agro-industry who need to be shame-faced now.[3] The iron winter of the industrial era is beginning its end. It is March all over the world, and now that a few crocuses are coming up through the snow, perhaps we can take heart to wait out the thirty-six years of coldness and death that remain before the New Age is in full blossom.

In this moment of late winter, we can see that pre-industrial and post-industrial are coming together to put an end to industrial civilization. The landscape of the New Age is not a regressive *Crunchy Granola* fantasy of nineteenth-century American agrarian life. We are not going back to what Marx called "the idiocy of rural life"; we are going back to nature with the consciousness of civilization behind us and the adventure of planetization in front of us. Urbanization and nationalism have reached their limits to growth along with industrialization, so the culture of the presently emerging future is one of decentralization of cities, miniaturization of technology and planetization of nations. In the twenty-first century, the trees shall be great, the buildings small, and the miniature machines in just proportion to man. Animism and electronics is the landscape of the New Age, and animism and electronics is already the landscape of Findhorn.

The return of animism to the West comes just in time, for with the consciousness that comes of animism we can truly humanize our technology. We certainly cannot humanize technology with behavioral science, and no one argues against himself more persuasively than the technocrat.

> According to Simon Ramo, founder of TRW, a successful high-technology firm, technology is an instrument for predicting the future and solving social problems. Because man "must now plan on sharing the earth with machines," he must "alter the rules of society, so that we and they can be compatible."[4]

To manage men, you have to process them the way you do tomatoes: grow plastic varieties that can endure machine harvesting and pick them when they are green and unripe. The kind of men who can live compatibly with their machines are very much like the food they eat. Ramo is not talking about humanizing technology, he is talking about technologizing man.

Simon Ramo and others like him at TRW and SRI will try to alter the rules of society by using the policy sciences to program a new form of cultural management. Through an interlocking directorate of multinational corporations, labor unions, government, foundations and universities, the Managers will point to the chaos they have created and appeal for special emergency powers to enable them to deal with the crisis through computer modeling and systems theory. And so, industrial civilization, like winter in March, will die hard. But I don't believe that the problem-solvers can win out in the long run of cultural evolution, for all their dream-solutions become even greater nightmare problems. Problem-solvers, with their artificial intelligence and machine-language, cannot tolerate ambiguity; they, therefore, cannot appreciate that organic forms generate life and culture, but that systems generate their linked-opposite of chaos. Thus the next ten years is likely to be a world of systems and chaos, the world of the Manager and the unmanageable Terrorist. Enjoy the crocuses of Findhorn, but keep your overcoat on.

The people of Findhorn understand the place of technology in nature, and if they forget, the elves will soon let them know that the human parking lots are stepping on their toes. Modern man knows how to talk back to nature, but he doesn't know how to listen. Archaic man knew how to listen to wind and water, flower and tree, angel and elf. All the archaic cultures, Tibetan, Hopi, Sufi and Celtic, are returning because they contain the very consciousness we need for the present and the future. The planetization of all the archaic cultures is coming at a time when it is desperately needed if we are going to evolve beyond the crisis of industrial civilization. Cultural evolution is not "being left to religion and the humanities," it is being led by religion and the humanities. And in evolution, flexibility, risk-taking and generalized adaptability count for more than bigness and strength. There is a weakness to bigness and power, and all the little cultures have returned to tell us that. The giant aerospace companies of Ramo's Los Angeles, or Sony's Tokyo are in trouble. Once the great apes chased us out of the trees into the dangerous savannahs, where, unable to swing happily where the great apes gibbered, we had to stoop down to pick up rocks. Now, the great apes are still back there in the trees. A new race of bullies in TRW and SRI and DOD are trying to push us around, and yet they are really pushing us out of materialism into the etheric dimension of a new adaptation.

And so the spiral of history turns; as we move away from industrial society, we come close to the animism of pre-industrial cultures. Whether it is an American Indian at Oraibi, or a scholarly gentleman in a Georgian flat in Edinburgh, it is a vision that belongs to us, our future as well as our past. If we had taken our Shakespeare seriously, we might not have had to travel half way round the world to discover the truth of Ariel's song.

> Where the bee sucks, there suck I
> In a cowslip's bell I lie;
> There I couch when owls do cry
> On the bat's back I do fly
> After summer merrily.
> Merrily, merrily shall I live now
> Under the blossom that hangs on the bough.

William Irwin Thompson

1. *Changing Images of Man,* Policy Report 4, The Center for the Study of Social Policy, Stanford Research Institute (Menlo Park, California, May 1974), p. 143.

2. Ibid., p. 17.

3. *See* John Todd, "The Dilemma Beyond Tomorrow," *The Journal of the New Alchemists,* 1974, pp. 122-8.

4. Richard J. Barnett and Ronald E. Muller, *Global Reach: the Power of the Multinational Corporations* (New York: Simon & Schuster, 1974), p. 338.

BYD 739

In the garden we feel
that we are indeed pioneers . . .
we are learning the very secrets of creation.

MAN CREATES THE GARDEN: PART 1. If I had stopped to question what we were doing or where we were going rather than proceeding in faith, step-by-step, the Findhorn garden could not have come into being. Certainly, the Findhorn Bay Caravan Park would have been the last place I would have chosen to live, least of all to start a garden. Driving past it on my way to Findhorn village, I had often thought "Fancy living in a place like that, cheek by jowl in those tiny caravans." Yet one snowy November day in 1962, I found myself moving our thirty-foot caravan trailer onto a site there. The six of us—my wife Eileen and myself, our three boys,

Christopher, Jonathan and David, and our colleague Dorothy Maclean—were to live in that small caravan for the next seven years. One day on the sand of this caravan park a garden would flourish and, eventually, a thriving spiritual community of nearly 200 people. We knew none of this at the time. We only knew that we had been led to this place by the guidance Eileen received in meditation.

During the previous ten years every action of our lives had been directed by this guidance from the voice of God within. If we were faithful to it we knew all our needs would be met and the nature of our work at Findhorn revealed.

For five years before moving into that caravan at Findhorn, I had been the manager of a large nearby hotel. During our time there, the hotel had trebled its financial takings and risen from a three- to a four-star rating—all in accord with the direct guidance of God. You can imagine, then, what it was like to come from the lap of luxury—with our five-course dinner each night—to this caravan surrounded by gorse and broom, sitting

on sand between a rubbish dump and a dilapidated garage.

I was unemployed, with no prospects of a job, and the six of us were living on eight pounds (about twenty dollars) a week Unemployment Benefit. Looking at the facts alone, our situation was a disaster. However, the arduous spiritual training Eileen, Dorothy and I had undergone in our lives enabled us to accept this extraordinary state of affairs. We had learned to surrender everything, including our wills, to God. Thus, when we were told that what we were doing at Findhorn would be of importance to the world, that there was a pattern and plan behind it, impossible as this seemed considering our circumstances, we accepted it. When guidance told us not only to live in the moment but to enjoy it, that is what we set out to do.

The boys reveled in the freedom of beaches to play on after the restrictions of a large hotel. The rest of us found the situation a challenge, an opportunity to apply the spiritual training we had received. One of the key lessons I had been given was to love wherever you are, whomever you are with and whatever you are doing. So I set to work to improve our surroundings, painting the inside and, when weather permitted, the outside of the caravan, as well as building an annex for Dorothy. Meanwhile, I went round for job interviews, certain that I would soon receive a position and we would move from the caravan park. Each week I queued up at the Labor Exchange with my former employees to collect my eight pounds. Personal pride never became an issue because I knew that what I was doing was right and in the divine plan. That was the only thing that mattered to me.

The weeks of unemployment grew into months, the months into years, and I moved from Unemployment Benefit to National Assistance. Each time a job came up I did as guidance told me and went for an interview, but always something happened to prevent me from getting it, to the ever-increasing consternation of the authorities. At one point, after about four years of this, a lot of publicity arose in the Press about lay-abouts on National Assistance not doing enough to get themselves a job, with the result that I was asked to come before a special committee.

They learned from my record that I had been a senior officer in the Royal Air Force, manager of a prestige hotel, that I was a good organizer, efficient and extremely healthy. Then why was I without a job? Eventually, the Board sent one of their investigators around to see me. He had with him a fat file with a complete record of my efforts to obtain employment. After going through it, he looked up at me and said, "Would you say that God is preventing you from getting a job?" Amazed at his understanding, I replied. "Why, yes, indeed." "Well," he said, "then presumably if we cut off your money, God will provide for you."

He had played his ace card. "Yes...yes, I expect... yes, he would." So that is what they did, and that is what God did. Just when they cut off the last payment, donations started coming in to us from our first publication of Eileen's guidance, *God Spoke to Me* which we had sent out to a small mailing list.

I started my first garden at Findhorn with no intention of it becoming a major project. While I had always been interested in gardening, I had actually done very little. Throughout our first winter in the caravan park, I spent the evenings and bad weather days poring over garden books of every conceivable point of view—organic and nonorganic, traditional and progressive—looking forward to a time when I might start my own garden. However, to create a garden there at Findhorn seemed as absurd as Noah building an ark where there was no water. We were situated on a narrow sandy peninsula jutting into the North Sea waters of the Moray Firth and were exposed to near-constant winds from all sides with only a belt of conifers to the west to provide shelter.

Worst of all was the soil: just sand and gravel held together by couch grass.

Despite this, by springtime of 1963, since I was still without a job, I decided to begin a small garden. I erected a woven wooden fence on one side of the caravan to stop the sand from seeping in at the door and to give us a private place to sit outside. Inside this, I planned to lay a concrete square for a patio and leave a small patch, eleven feet by six feet, to grow a few radishes and lettuce.

With no money to purchase the cement for this patio, we had to proceed in faith, knowing our needs would be met. As Eileen's guidance had told us: *Consider how I fed the children of Israel with manna from Heaven. Forty years in the wilderness I did it for them. Why should not your every need be met? Are you not My chosen children? Have I not laid My hand upon you? Believe that all things are possible and make them so.*

Always remember, it was their daily needs I met. Therefore, never hoard anything. Whatever you have, use as a gift from Me and know there is plenty more where that came from. My gifts are unending, for all is Mine. Whenever you attempt to put something away for a rainy day, remember this, and you will cease looking ahead, you will cease looking behind, and you will live to the full, now. As your needs are met, give constant thanks.

We went ahead and cleared an area for cementing. Sure enough, a few days later a neighbor came to tell us that a truck had just left a whole load of cement in bags, slightly damaged by water, in the dump across the road. Though it may seem an astounding coincidence, events like this had become normal in our lives. We could only be thankful and proceed. I collected several tons of the cement in the back of my car and completed the patio and a slab of concrete around the caravan.

I hadn't found my winter research into gardening exactly encouraging. Most of the books, besides containing discrepancies, had been written for gardens in the south of England where the growing season and climate are far more favorable than they are in northeast Scotland. Furthermore, they were written for gardens with *soil,* and clearly what we had here was sand with a mass of stones and gravel about a foot below.

To prepare for planting I had to remove the turf, a tangle of couch grass. I turned this upside down into the bottom of trenches eighteen inches wide by one foot deep and chopped it up thoroughly. Then the fine sand was replaced on top. We found the soil so dry that water formed bubbles on the top and ran off. Despite this, we sowed our first seeds.

At this time a job turned up which I thought I had a reasonable chance of landing, but again, somehow, it fell through. Eileen was very concerned about this recurring situation, but she received the guidance: *It is not right for Peter to have a job yet, but he must be willing to go for the interviews. You need not give them any force, and it will not come about. When he goes for interviews, he will have to let Me guide him in action.* It seems I was being asked to concentrate on the garden and my work there. I decided to cultivate the area between the wooden fence and the garage. As there were a lot of rabbits about, I put up a wire fence to protect the plants and prepared the earth in the same way as before, only this time adding manure collected from a nearby riding stable. As time went on and prospective jobs fell through, I continued to add to the garden.

Behind the garage was a piece of ground I could cultivate with enough extra space for compost heaps, which I felt were vital. During April I tackled this area and started collecting ingredients for compost. As with every other part of the garden, my training in positive thought and reliance on God—put into action through hard work—brought us everything we needed to transform the barren soil.

We were off to a good start when we learned that a bale of straw had fallen off a truck on a nearby road. I jumped into my car and set out to find it. On the way back, I saw a young man whom I knew walking along the road and offered him a lift. Feeling a bit foolish with straw lying on the back seat of the car, I explained that I needed it for a compost heap I was starting. "Well," he said, "you know that field we just passed at the end of the road with horses in it. Why don't you take the horse manure from there for your compost?" "But I don't know the people who own those horses," I replied. He said, "I own them." The next day we all went down in the car with bins, buckets and an old tin bath to collect horse manure for the compost heap.

The owner of the caravan park delivered grass cuttings by the load. A shop in town gave us old potatoes and vegetables too spoiled to be sold. Dorothy and Eileen cut seaweed off the rocks on the shore by Findhorn village. This was cold, hard work but compost was vital to the garden.

Another crucial ingredient was potash which comes from the ashes of wood fires. Since our only fuel was coal, I was constantly on the lookout for possible sources of wood ash. Whenever I saw smoke go up on the horizon, from fires connected with tree felling, off I would go to see what might be collected. Every single ingredient in that compost gave us not only additional nutriment for the soil but an adventure as well. The love and appreciation we felt for each item we collected was itself a major contribution to the compost.

Our other needs in the garden were met in the same way. For example, in exchange for helping a neighbor to dismantle old garages, he gave us wood for fences and frames to protect tender plants from the cold and wind. Within the frames we created hotbeds, using fresh horse manure mixed with straw and leaves for heat. You can imagine the amazement of the local people at the sight of three adults—Dorothy, Eileen and myself—back out in the fields again, this time following horses with shovels and buckets to collect that precious, fresh manure. No wonder strange stories go around about the Findhorn community!

Next, I tackled the steep slope covered with gorse and brambles behind the caravan. Digging into it, I found nothing more than gravel. There was hardly even sand. The soil had washed down the slope and settled between the caravan and the garage. The only answer was to exchange the two, wheelbarrowing gravel out, shoveling soil in. This involved an enormous amount of work, but it had a spiritual as well as physical effect on the area. I was told that by working in total concentration and with love for what I was doing, I could instill light into the soil. It is difficult to explain, but I was actually aware of radiations of light and love passing through me as I worked. This did not happen until I got a spade in my hands and started digging. Then, like connecting up negative and positive poles in electricity, the energy flowed through me into the soil. This work was transforming the area and creating an intangible wall of light, like a force field, around the caravan.

When this area of the garden was prepared, I planted it with leeks and celery, rutabagas (called swedes in Britain) and turnips, more radishes and lettuce, peas and beans and a few other vegetables.

Our days were interspersed with times of quiet, inner activity. When the weather permitted, we meditated on the patio. Both Eileen and Dorothy wrote down the guidance they received each day from the God within. This ranged from advice on inner development, to the food we were to eat, to specific tasks for the day. My own guidance took the form of intuitive flashes of inspiration—often received while working—that carried a sense of conviction, a deep inner knowing. These were sometimes confirmed and amplified by the guidance Eileen received. One of the advantages of working as a group was that our personal guidance could be checked with the others when there was any doubt as to whether it was coming from the lower self, or from a higher level. When we all felt the same inner knowing, it was right to proceed.

Of the three of us, Dorothy had always had the closest link with nature. One morning in May, a couple of months after we had first started the garden, she received a message during meditation that brought us into a totally new phase in the garden's development. She directly contacted a spirit of the plant kingdom, the deva of the garden pea. We knew the devas to be that part of the angelic hierarchy that holds the archetypal pattern for each plant species and directs energy toward bringing a plant into form on the physical plane. During my spiritual training, I had been made aware of the nature forces, particularly the "elementals," the spirits of earth, air, fire and water. To me, devas and nature spirits were an integral part of the creative process, the life force personified. In fact, at one time, I had been very interested in conscious cooperation with them. Now, here was the Pea Deva offering to help us in our garden. I jumped at the chance, thinking: At last! Now we can get straight from the horse's mouth the answers to any questions we have on gardening. I brought out all those questions that had stumped us over the past several weeks as our gardens began to grow, and Dorothy put them to the deva of the species concerned. Strange as it may seem, we received the answers. Practical answers to practical questions.

They told us how far apart plants should be, how often to water them, what was wrong and what to do about it. These were just straightforward gardening answers that any gardener might know. The point was, *we* didn't know them. Moreover, the devas told us that this kind of conscious cooperation between man and the nature forces was a pioneering experiment for them as well, and together we discovered some methods of gardening that went beyond the normal practices. For example, after I had sown our first lettuce seeds, I did as the garden books advised, thinning the rows and planting out the thinnings to make five or six rows out of the original one. But most of our transplanted lettuce started dying, and we didn't know why. When Dorothy asked the Lettuce Deva what to do, we were told it would be better to sow seeds thickly in each row, then eliminate those that are weak, rather than transplant. We could recycle the life force in them through the compost. This proved to be sound advice.

However, when this work first began, it caused a certain tension between Dorothy and myself. Beautiful messages or guidance from God were of no use, I felt, unless they could be applied in daily life. However, contacting the various devas was delicate work, and she needed to relate to their light, transcendent realms. I, of course, was more down-to-earth, pestering her for hard-core practical advice for the garden. Eventually, we got the right balance, when we realized that in order to "bring it down here" she had to "go up there." But both aspects were essential—the spiritual and the practical. To create Heaven on Earth, as we were told to do, it was necessary to be firmly grounded in both worlds.

It is the same in cooperating with the devic realms. Man does not forego his own powers and abilities, approaching the devas as if helpless, expecting them to supply the answers. Not at all. Man contributes his part to the work as an equal, and the devas respond by contributing theirs. True cooperation begins when we realize that man, the devas and nature spirits are part of the same life force, creating together. As a representative of man in the garden, I accepted communications from the devas as advice yet knew that I must create the garden as I saw fit, considering the available time, workers, weather and material resources. The ultimate choice of action on this planet always rests with man. This sometimes meant we could not put into immediate practice what we were receiving and learning from them, but our conscious cooperation with the nature kingdoms was beginning.

The devas were teaching us not only how to supply the material needs of plants, but also how to perceive the plants' true nature. We were asked to see the world around us in terms of the life force or energy behind the outward form. As the devas told us, *In our world, which is closer to the world of causes, we see that all things are a manifestation of intelligence and that all happenings are related. If you put the horse before the cart, all power will be in your hands and you will work in the world of forces as we do.* The devas told us that, because our thoughts and states of mind affected the garden, one of the most vital contributions we could make was the radiation we put into the soil while cultivating it and the love we gave to the plants while tending them. This love, rather than a sentimental emotion, was the ability to be truly sensitive to the needs, both material and spiritual, of the plants in our garden.

Something very strange was happening in our lives. I was being mysteriously prevented from getting a job so that all my time and energy were going into creating this garden. Now we were establishing a relationship with the devas who had previously been so shy of modern man with his destructive ways. Why all this concentration on the garden? One morning during meditation, it struck me. We were pioneering something new. Twentieth-century Western man was consciously working, hand-in-hand, with the spiritual aspects of the nature kingdoms. That evening Eileen received in guidance: *Tell Peter that what illuminated him this morning was indeed so. You are working with nature, with the devas and elementals, and are gradually finding harmony with them. What is now happening is something new, and this is the way the world is to be re-created. You are all learning the secret of creation in your various ways.*

Now we began to understand why we had had to leave the hotel where everything on the material level was provided. We were preparing to live in a new consciousness and had to learn, once and for all, the power of man to create his own world. We are all capable of bringing about what we set our minds to if it is for the good of the whole. Our work was to create a perfect garden in cooperation with nature. Normally, to create such a garden would require a good deal of money, and we had neither salary nor bank balance. What we did have was what anybody else anywhere could have—ourselves, our positive thoughts and faith in God's unlimited abundance. In learning to see the world in terms of causes rather than effects, we had to rely on God as the source of all supply rather than looking to a salary and bank balance for security. The principles we were working with in this were not new; they are part of the ancient wisdoms, but they have no reality unless they are lived and proved. This time of unemployment was the perfect opportunity to put them into practice.

In June, 1963, Eileen received: *You realize, at last, that no longer need you be controlled by events, but by your power of thought you control them. You can bring about anything by your thoughts. That is why this new-found power can only be used when there is no self left to mar it; otherwise it could so easily be used for the wrong motive and not for the good of the whole. Used by that higher part of you, only good can be drawn to you and you can create only good.*

This is the secret of creation. What you think, you create. This is where your faith and belief must be unshakable. When there are any doubts or lack of confidence, you are unable to bring about these truths in form.

My wonders are to be manifest in form. Heaven is to be brought on Earth. We are one. Therefore, all that appeared impossible in the past is no longer so. Everything is possible.

It had seemed miraculous that all our needs were being met. Yet this was not really a miracle at all; it was the natural result of working in accordance with the very laws upon which creation is based.

We were frequently assured in guidance that the work we were doing was vital for the future and that it extended beyond the garden. Whenever we wondered or questioned, we were reminded to think of Noah: *The garden is like the ark I asked Noah to build. It is difficult for you to see the reason for it, for you cannot see into the future, but let Me assure you that it is vitally important. Every single thing that is put into it is vital. Everything must be done under My guidance, with the help and cooperation of the devas and nature spirits. This is a work to unite and make whole that which has been sorely torn and divided.* Slowly, we were beginning to perceive the significance of our work in the garden.

By the end of May I had begun working on the last uncultivated area next to the caravan. This piece of land on the east side was sand and turf filled with wireworms. A lot of time and energy, love and nutrients were needed to bring life to this dead soil. Besides compost, I added cummins (barley sprouts from a nearby distillery), peat, lime—and a good sprinkling of soot to deter the wireworms who would eat anything sown or planted. When all this had been mixed into the soil we were told by the devas to let the new piece of land rest for a while before planting in it. *Any new addition to the garden has to be brought into the whole. The garden is a definite unit, and a little time is needed to properly embrace a new section into its heart.*

By the first week of June this soil was planted. Our caravan now sat in the midst of a garden.

We were already eating the first fruits of our labor—radishes, lettuce and turnips. But we were also beginning to confront a great number of challenges. The tomatoes were suffering from the cold and lack of sun. The newly sprouted onions were struck by a damping-off disease. The leaves of the broad beans shot up and then flopped. This was due to the poor quality of the soil, the devas told us. They suggested taking out the weak ones to give the others what sustenance there was in the soil and told us that our positive thoughts could contribute to the strength of the plants.

Then, of course, there was "other life" in the garden, such as cabbage root fly. We discovered that most of our cabbage crop was wilting and dying because a grub was eating the roots. The devas told us to think of the plants as strong, healthy and leafy, while they would charge them with sufficient life to withstand the attacks. We drew soil up around the stems and poured love into them. In other gardens in the area, cabbages died. Those in our garden managed to hang on until the larvae had eaten all the roots below and had gone into chrysalids. Then the plants developed new roots higher up where we had put the soil and continued to grow.

I had never realized how many obstacles a plant had to overcome to reach maturity. However, I took what was happening in the garden as a challenge, to get over or around, to learn from. Yet sometimes it really seemed hopeless to rely on organic methods for fertilizing the soil and protecting the plants against insects. The whole environment seemed to be out of balance, and how could one small garden function naturally within that? The devas told us that much of the imbalance had been caused by man, killing off the birds who fed on insects, for example, by using poisonous insecticides or by filling the atmosphere with chaotic thoughts and unnatural atomic radiations. (This was during a time when many nuclear weapons were being tested in different parts of the world.) As we put life into the soil, they told us, and refrained from using those materials which destroy life, we were working to right the balance. The devas offered us their special assistance.

Thus, despite all the challenges, the garden thrived. By the end of June it was starting to attract local attention. People would come to have a look and go away shaking their heads, scarcely able to believe it was only three months since the first seeds were sown. How could there be so much greenness and vitality when all around was dry deadness? Of course, we couldn't tell them about the help and cooperation of the devas. People thought us strange enough as it was. As the life force developed in the soil, the plants thrived and rapidly became resistant to disease and pests. All life processes in the garden were being speeded up. The devas told us: *In terms of life force, the improvement in the soil is tremendous. Not only have you worked as few humans have ever worked, but we, too, have had a constant rain of radiations pouring into the soil. It has been a combined effort and because of the push of it, the results are much faster than normal.*

Being continually in the garden as we were, we just accepted it, not fully realizing how overflowing with abundance and vitality it was. Then one Sunday afternoon we went to visit the gardens of nearby Cawdor Castle, which had been cultivated for several hundred years by professional gardeners. We were amazed to see that our vegetables were actually much larger and in better condition than theirs. With gratitude, we began to realize the effects of cooperation with the devas.

The garden was becoming the mainstay of our vegetarian diet. That summer of 1963, Eileen began receiving specific instructions on refining our bodies through eating our own produce. We were told that the foods we were growing in the garden with the help of the devas and nature spirits were filled with the life force that our bodies needed.

Not only our diet but physical exercise as well was important in our lives. I was told through Eileen's guidance: *My son, it is most important to keep your physical body fit and healthy so I can use you at any time to do anything for Me. Some form of exercise is needed daily. What you do is not as important as doing it each day. You do not know what I have need of you to do for Me, but I can assure you that I have much and you will need to be in perfect health to do it. Now it's up to you.*

Little did I know what lay ahead of me over the next years. I went for long runs along the beach every day, finishing off with a plunge into the invigorating waters of the Moray Firth. I did indeed become physically fit.

None too soon, for that autumn we encountered a true challenge, not romantic but certainly vital—picking potatoes, or "tatties," as they are called here. By this time, we had used up the manure supply in the neighboring field, and we still needed more. It is, of course, a cosmic law that when one door closes, another opens. I had often noted that there was a huge pile of manure on the farm next door to us. It sat there idly year after year while the farmer used the artificial fertilizers subsidized by the British government. I decided to go to see him about it.

It was October and potato harvesting time, so I offered him the services of Dorothy and myself picking potatoes in exchange for manure. The farmer felt we were getting the worst of the bargain, but I assured him that we'd be quite happy to work if we could have as much manure as we could cart away. Being short of labor, he agreed.

But first we had to pay the price. It was really agony bending down all day for two weeks, picking tatties, but it was worth it for the sake of the garden. Over the next three months, much to the surprise and chagrin of the farmer, we carried the entire pile of manure away in buckets, tin tubs and dustbins in the back of my car.

As it turned out, this hard-earned manure not only provided valuable fertilizer, but it also exposed us for the first time to devic humor. I had decided to start growing mushrooms, one of the few crops we did not have in the garden. Attempting to do everything perfectly, we got fresh horse manure and prepared it by laboriously turning it several times, read books and followed the instructions with utmost accuracy. We even bought a thermometer to take the temperature of the horse manure—a high extravagance in those days. Dorothy contacted the Mushroom Deva who said we would see "astonishing results." In passing, Dorothy mentioned that this deva had felt sort of round and as if it had a sense of humor.

We did everything for those mushrooms, carefully putting some in the garage and some under frames. All the while the Mushroom Deva was reminding us: *Growth depends on many factors which we cannot foretell, and therefore we—any of us—always grow where possible.* More care went into looking after those mushrooms than anything else we had ever grown. After all, we were expecting astonishing results. After weeks and weeks of this, our mushroom beds produced two tiny offspring. But all over the garden where that four-year-old horse manure had been spread was a magnificent crop of mushrooms!

Winter was coming again, and we were still at Findhorn. What were we supposed to do now? The guidance Eileen was given in December, 1963 clarified this: *I want you to look upon this place as a permanent home and know that all the effort that is put into it will bear an abundance of fruit, not only material fruit but spiritual fruit as well. Remember, this is a vast work. Peter will need the help and cooperation of each one of you to bring it about on all levels. It is only when you seek that you find; therefore, never sit back and expect anything to fall into your lap.*

I had no doubts as to my next course of action. To the south of our caravan, outside the patio fence, was a whole area of land not being used for caravan sites because it was too sloping and uneven.

With the permission of the caravan park owner, I planned a garden for that area. In February and March, when the ground had sufficiently thawed, I set to work preparing the soil. Along the fence I planted berry bushes and cordon-grown apples. Besides giving us fruit, they would provide a living, protective wall, radiating light and beauty.

The aims of the garden were becoming clearer. Guidance told us: *You are to have as many varieties of fruits and vegetables as possible. Contact with the devas is essential, and this can only be done when each plant is actually grown.*

The devas themselves told us they liked variety in the garden, because each plant added its unique radiation and because as many devas as possible wanted to participate in our experiment. While gardening books advise adding only three or four new species to the garden each year, we were welcoming them in by the dozen. In fact, during

1964, we grew sixty-five different types of vegetables, twenty-one kinds of fruits and forty-two different herbs. As we sowed seeds or set out young plants, Dorothy welcomed the deva of each. Like Noah's ark for the animals, our garden was beginning to gather a representative selection of the plant life that could be grown in our part of the world.

We found that our expanded and overflowing garden was requiring a great deal of hard work. I was kept busy from dawn until dusk, and in this land near the midnight sun, those summer days were indeed long. Dorothy joined me in the morning and Eileen in the afternoon, digging, building paths, making fences and frames, creating hotbeds, gathering materials for the compost, turning the heaps, making liquid manure, sowing, planting, thinning, weeding, watering, encouraging, loving. Every square inch of soil was handled by each of us several times. Every plant we invited into the garden was given the environment and conditions in which it could best express its life. With all this work, we retired to bed at night physically tired but in a state of complete relaxation, because we knew that we were fulfilling the divine plan.

I had the overall vision for the development and needs of the garden. Yet it was equally important that others work in it as well. Eileen's guidance pointed out to us: *You are all to help as much as you can. You must remember that the more you all put into the soil by way of radiations the better. You each have a certain something to contribute to the whole. This is not just Peter's garden, it belongs to all of you.*

It was pinpointed concentration in each moment that was needed to create the garden. I focused all my energy on it, thinking about little else. I found that with this attitude it was possible to let my intuition guide me in the work. For years as part of my spiritual training, I had been learning to follow and trust those inner promptings. Of course, mistakes were made, but they always taught me something. I saw that listening solely to the rational mind would bog me down with reasons, pros and cons, on every action. So I tried to tune into the voice of the higher mind and plunge into action. Soon enough I discovered whether I had responded to true intuition or merely to the desires of the separative personality. Gradually I learned to distinguish between the two. Eileen received guidance supporting this intuitive way of working: *My son, let the garden develop naturally. When you are in the middle of something and suddenly feel that it is right to place a certain vegetable in a certain place, do so, even if it means changing everything around again. The garden is rather like a crossword puzzle, and when you get the right plant in the right place, you will see where the next plant should go. Now, this may not be the usual way of gardening, but this is not the usual garden. You will find that the whole garden will develop as you carry on and do one thing at a time, without too many rigid plans.*

Ultimately, since it is love that fulfills all laws, it was my love for the garden that put me in tune with it. I remember one year we had several thousand annuals sown in boxes, waiting to be set out. When it came to planting them, I really didn't know what the various plants were. I laid out the boxes in three rows—tall, medium and short plants. Then I planted a patch of this here and a patch of that there, as I was prompted in the moment. The outcome was such that when a gardening expert, one who specialized in annuals, later came to visit, he said, "I've never seen such a beautiful display of annuals. What a lot of time and effort must have gone into planning it." As far as the beauty of it was concerned, he was right; the colors and forms blended in perfectly. But I did have to admit to him that I hadn't planned it at all.

In 1964, our second season, the garden was literally overflowing with life. The devas and nature spirits were outdoing themselves not only in quality—the produce was filled with amazing vitality and flavor—but in quantity as well. At the beginning of the season, I had estimated the number of red cabbages we would need for the year. At the average weight of four pounds, we would require about eight. But when those red cabbages reached maturity, they were so large that one weighed 38 pounds and another 42. It was the same with a white sprouting broccoli which grew to such proportions that it fed us for months. When I eventually pulled it up, it was nearly too heavy to lift.

Certainly this was beyond the natural pattern for these vegetables. Considering what we had been told over and over about the power of thoughts, perhaps our enthusiasm contributed to the energy and growth there. We did, indeed, do everything with great zest in the garden. It may also have been that something spectacular was needed to draw attention to our garden, to pave the way for a time when we might openly talk about our conscious cooperation with devas and nature spirits.

Because we were constantly in the midst of it, we didn't actually think too much about what was happening. We didn't even think to take photographs of these early phenomena. Then Eileen received the following, commenting on what was happening: *You are in a fully protected area where you can put into practice and bring about My wonders. You can create by your right thinking. I have put you here in this place which is specially prepared and protected so you can learn to make My Word live, so you can learn to bring about the truths I have been telling you for a very long time. Now you are beginning to see them manifest in form, brought down from those higher realms so you can behold them with your own eyes.*

Like an artist, stand back every now and again and survey the work you are doing from a distance. Otherwise you may fail to realize what is going on. You are so close to it, so on top of it. Remember, everything is very concentrated here, everything is pinpointed. You are living in the middle of a powerhouse and can fail to realize the terrific power that radiates from this area.

Everything we did was serving to increase the energies of light here. We recycled through the compost all unused scraps from the kitchen, as well as our own body wastes. The devas told us that, since our bodies did not have the usual impurities in them that modern man living in cities had, it was safe for us to do so. Because we didn't have flush toilets then, we could empty the contents of our night buckets onto the compost heaps each day together with straw. Thus the energy was contained and built up within the area, creating a spiritual as well as a physical whole. (Now, with the expanded community, our compost uses only garden and green kitchen wastes.)

With so much growing in such a limited space, ours was a very intensive garden. During the early summer of 1964, I had been strongly prompted to plant out thousands of seedling lettuce, not really considering what could be done with them since we could not possibly use such a vast quantity. We had lettuce everywhere, between radishes and fruit trees, along celery trenches, planted on each ridge. The entire garden was a mass of brilliant green.

As it happened, there was a shortage of lettuce in the area that year and individuals and shops came from far and wide to buy ours, as well as our spinach, parsley and radishes. The taste of organically grown vegetables and the quality of produce from this special garden accounted for the speed with which the word went round. With the money from the sales we were able to buy more seeds and plants for the garden.

That autumn we began a fruit garden. As we put in each plant, Dorothy contacted the deva of that species. All expressed great excitement in joining us, and with their help we hoped to grow apple, pear, plum and even peach and apricot trees; bushes of greengages, cherries, black currants, red currants, gooseberries, raspberries, boysenberries and loganberries; and a large patch of strawberries in the vegetable garden between the patio and garage. Despite our determination and the willingness of the devas, the growing season here wasn't long enough to allow the peach, apricot and pear trees to bear fruit. The devas have said that man one day will have the ability to control weather conditions but only when he has a deeper understanding of the wholeness of life.

The other trees and bushes produced fruit abundantly. In fact, the story eventually came back to us from London that strawberries weighing a pound each were growing at Findhorn. The strawberries were indeed huge, but what I actually had said was that the plants were prolific enough to provide us with a pound of strawberries each per day. It just goes to show that people hear what they want to.

This remarkable abundance continued throughout the next summer as well. As we took visitors around the garden, it was interesting to note how most assumed we were using artificial fertilizers in order to obtain such growth, as if nature alone were not capable of this. It certainly made us realize the power of conscious cooperation with the nature forces. But we still did not talk to visitors about our work with devas and nature spirits. However, I soon did find myself in the position of having to explain publicly what was happening in our garden.

In autumn of 1965, I asked the County Horticultural Adviser to come and take a soil sample. I felt it was time we got some expert gardening advice on the varieties of plants best suited to this soil and climate. I admit that I felt the soil must be lacking in some ingredients, even though the devas had told us that if the soil was deficient, they, with the help of the nature spirits, could produce from the ethers the elements needed for perfect growth. The adviser's first comment on arriving was that he knew this type of soil well and that it would certainly require a dressing of at least two ounces of sulphate of potash per square yard. I pointed out that I did not believe in artificial fertilizers and that I had been using the ashes of wood fires as a source of potash. For the next two hours he explained why wood ash could not come anywhere near satisfying the soil and that a few other ingredients would be necessary as well. He nearly convinced me.

He took away samples of the soil to be analyzed and returned six weeks later, baffled. The analysis had found no deficiencies whatsoever. All necessary elements were present. He was so impressed that he asked if I would take part in a radio broadcast on our garden, with him refereeing a discussion between myself and a professional gardener, well-experienced in broadcasting, who advocated conventional chemical methods of gardening. I agreed.

On the program he asked me what had accounted for the growth of the produce in our garden. He himself had seen the astonishing size, color and vigor of our plants. Not feeling that the public was yet ready for talk about devas and such, I attributed it to the use of compost, organic gardening methods and hard work. However, I did use the opportunity to voice my opinion that the whole balance of nature was being upset by man who was now beginning to reap the results of what he had sown. Hopefully, our garden was seen as a way to help mend the situation.

In response to the soil analysis, the devas told us: *We knew that this garden would confound the experts, because it is not like other gardens. Yes, we can and do draw unto ourselves what is needed in our work from the everlasting life substance. This process is speeded up when the material we need is available to us in a form easier for us to use, that is, when it has already been converted previously. This, of course, is where your cooperation in putting materials into the soil makes all the difference to the plants.*

This process is also easier for us when your creative power is flowing to the land, when what is coming from you is of the highest. Man counteracts our work not only by the poisons he purposefully puts forth but also by the many ways in which he breaks cosmic law in his selfishness. When all is more or less in line, as in this garden, our creation forges ahead not only unimpeded but accelerated.

Thus nineteen months after our first garden had been created, the results of our cooperation with the nature forces became apparent to us through more than just our experience. Now, we had the scientific evidence that something extraordinary was occurring in our garden.

Just at this point our faith was tested. Dorothy had begun working as a secretary in 1965 for a gentleman who owned a walled garden a few hundred years old. It had good soil, and was completely equipped with greenhouses, tools, everything a gardener might wish for. He offered it to us free, in exchange for keeping him supplied with fresh vegetables. That was tempting. But were we growing our garden merely for the produce? What of all the radiations we had been guided to instill in the soil? Clearly, from the rational point of view, we were foolish to refuse his offer, but we knew within ourselves we must have faith in God's guidance and continue at Findhorn.

However, our time of relative isolation was clearly over as word of our work began to spread. As we made contact with others involved in spiritual activities in Britain, our group grew to seven adult members. I found myself travelling from Findhorn every two or three months to visit people in Britain who I felt were on a similar spiritual path. Unknown to me, through several of these contacts, new phases of activity were to unfold in the garden.

There was one person I felt especially prompted to keep in touch with at that time—a very quiet man living in a book-lined apartment in Edinburgh, R. Ogilvie Crombie. I had been told that during his sixty-odd years he had not only delved into spiritual and occult knowledge, but was well versed in the sciences of physics, chemistry, psychology and parapsychology. He was an intriguing man.

In 1966 Roc, as we usually called him, came to Findhorn for the first time. Shortly after, he had an experience which proved to be a turning point in his life—and ours as well.

One afternoon when he was sitting in the Royal Botanic Gardens, Roc had his first visual encounter with a nature spirit, with whom he also conversed. Soon after this experience he had the first of several meetings with the nature god himself, Pan. He felt—and indeed was later told—that these meetings were directly linked to the part he had to play at Findhorn.

The garden clearly had become the focal point for an experiment in the cooperation of three kingdoms: the devic, the elemental and the human. Each of us at Findhorn was playing a distinct and necessary role in the experiment. Eileen received direct guidance from the voice of God within. Dorothy was in communication with the devas. Roc had the ability to see and speak with nature spirits. I was the representative of man, the active practical creator of the garden. Of necessity, in our individual roles, we did not always see eye to eye. But we were learning how these three kingdoms could work together to create a new world in accord with the divine plan.

The mistakes we made during the course of this experiment only served to point the way toward true cooperation between man and nature in the world today. If a man like myself who was not a gardener could, by consciously cooperating with the forces of nature, bring abundant life from sand, then men everywhere could re-create the earth—providing they followed certain principles. These we were working to discover.

Learning to work with the nature spirits kept us on our toes. While the devas are anxious to cooperate but are rather detached from the results of their work, the nature spirits are more susceptible to direct influence by man and thus can get upset when he interferes with their work. We soon had a nature spirit strike on our hands.

Between our caravan and the wild area of gorse and broom behind it is a small fruit orchard. By May, 1966, the gorse had grown right up around our apple trees and gooseberry bushes. I asked Dennis, a young man who had been with us for three or four months, to cut back the bushes that were interfering with the trees. Although he didn't like to do this to the gorse in flower, he explained to the nature spirits what had to be done, apologized and proceeded. Lena, one of our group, felt it was all wrong to cut them in flower. Dorothy

was almost in tears, saying I was butchering them. I retorted, "Oh, don't be so damned silly," feeling that these women were really going too far. "Every time you mow the lawn you're butchering it."

The next thing I knew Roc was telephoning from Edinburgh, asking me what had I been doing to upset the nature spirits in the garden. Is he mad? I thought. I haven't been doing anything. "Nothing," I replied. "Well, you have," he said, and he came up to Findhorn. That weekend with us, while crossing the moor covered with flowering gorse and broom, Roc found himself surrounded by a throng of little gorse elves all aflurry. "We thought Findhorn was a place where there was cooperation between man and the nature spirits. How, in Heaven's name, could they have done such an awful thing as destroy our homes?" The elves lived, so it seemed, in the blossoms of the gorse and broom. They told Roc that they had all left the garden and refused to work there any longer because of this thoughtless destruction. Roc explained that this had not been intentional, that the cooperation in the garden was, so to speak, comparatively new. Man was trying his best and he certainly would not deliberately do anything to upset them. Later, we held a little ceremony out by the offended bushes in which I expressed my profuse apologies. The elves understood and agreed to return. The strike was over.

This whole episode illustrated how I, as a representative of modern man, could override the sensitive feelings of others perhaps more instinctively close to nature—and in ignorance upset the nature spirits. Later Roc received the following message from a higher being: *Remind Peter that at Findhorn, where a pioneering experiment in cooperation between man, the devas and the nature forces is being carried out, the greatest care must be taken to refrain from any action that will give offence. This particularly applies to the nature spirits who are active in the garden. You cannot continue to expect cooperation from beings, many of whom still doubt that man deserves their help, though they are willing to make the experiment, if you do not respect their principles.*

There are certain practices common in many gardens which should not be used here. Peter, as master of the garden, is the one to make decisions. But he must be warned that if he makes a mistake serious consequences will result. Not only will the nature forces concerned depart from the garden, but a penalty will be imposed. This will be severe as there is now no excuse for offending these spirits. He can no longer plead ignorance.

Certain flower spirits left because of what seemed to them to be wanton mutilation of the plants they tend by removing the blossoms. Remember these spirits are concerned with beauty and resent any violation of it. Flowers may be picked to beautify the home. They will not resent this if it is explained to them. If flowers have to be pulled off in order to stimulate growth of leaves for food, for instance, this should be done before the flowers have opened out. Once they have done

so they may have become the dwelling places of tiny little beings whose presence and whose good-will ought to be cherished, not repulsed.

I had often been told by guidance to liken myself to Noah. Well, I could see this had two sides to it. Not only was Noah persevering and willing to follow God's guidance step-by-step, but you might also say he was headstrong and maybe a bit near-sighted. No sooner had we straightened things out with the gorse elves than I discovered that, hanging over one of our black currant bushes, almost smothering it, was a broom plant—in full bloom. "Ogilvie," I said, "that broom is killing the black currant which we need for food—vital Vitamin C and all. Surely the nature spirits will understand if I cut it back now." Roc just said, "Oh yes, I suppose they will."

When Roc consulted the nature spirits, all they had to tell me was: *Peter knows.* With the abstract air of a scientist about him, Roc said, "Why don't you go ahead and cut it—and see what happens?"

Then I remembered the gorse elves. What could I say? We'd just have to do without the black currants.

But the nature spirits had told Roc that if I left the bushes alone I wouldn't regret it; they would make it up to me. Although it was a poor year for black currants in the area, our bushes were overflowing. Eileen would groan every time I came into the kitchen with baskets of black currants, because it would mean having to make more preserves. The nature spirits had kept their side of the bargain. Since then we have only pruned or cut back plants when they are not in bloom.

We were learning a great deal about relating to plants with care. Both the devas and nature spirits had told us that plants should be forewarned whenever they are going to be picked, pruned, transplanted or otherwise worked with by man. Thus, in 1967 when the time came to build a greenhouse, we warned the gorse and broom growing on the site and then lovingly removed them. When we tried to level the area with a light-weight excavating machine, it just sank into the sand. Later, without my knowledge, one of our group got hold of a bulldozer and ripped through the area. The job was done, but what an uproar it brought from the nature spirits. We could all feel devastation in the air. Again we had learned. The earth itself is a living substance, inhabited by many nature beings who deserve consideration. They, too, need to be forewarned. Then an individual operating a machine with awareness can use it as an extension of himself to clear an area with love and care. Man's actions do not have to be destructive. With sensitivity, man can cooperate with nature to transform the world around him.

MAN CREATES THE GARDEN: PART 2. Our group continued to grow throughout 1966-67. People began to join us from different parts of the world. We now had several caravans, and prefabricated cedarwood bungalows were being erected. The garden continued as a source of food and any surplus was sold to the local people and to the increasing number of visitors. Then Eileen received guidance that the garden was to be extended and made into a place of beauty. For the first time we began to grow flowers.

The flowers we brought into our garden were also from around the world, and we worked to create the proper conditions for them. A greenhouse was constructed; rocks were transported from the surrounding countryside for a rock garden; a water garden and later a marsh garden were created. *We would have this garden represent the world, for we wish to have the cooperation of the world,* the devas told us. Although the environments we created were artificial in our geographical area, this was man choosing to re-create the earth—and the plants flourished. The flowers were literally radiant with light. Many of our visitors told us that they had never seen such a uniformly high standard in any garden before. They were at a loss to understand it in view of the poverty of the soil and the northern climate. Even the primula, the polyanthus, and other moisture-loving plants thrived in almost pure sand. Foxgloves, which normally grow to three and four feet in rich soil, grew to eight and nine

feet in our sandy garden. In the worst possible soil for roses, ours bloomed in perfection.

The time was coming closer when we would have to speak publicly about our work with the devas and nature spirits. It was Sir George Trevelyan, nephew of the noted historian G. M. Trevelyan, who actually saw the significance of what we were doing and himself began to spread the word. At Easter-time, 1968, he paid us his first visit.

Sir George is well-known for the part he played in initiating the adult education movement in England. His college at Attingham Park was also the scene of many conferences held on New Age themes. It was at one of these conferences for New Age group leaders, in 1965, that I first met him. Even though I was there merely as an observer, and our "New Age community" was externally little more than a few caravans surrounded by a garden, I was prompted to stand up and tell this imposing group that we were actually *living* the principles they were discussing. As a result, Sir George invited me to speak. During the discussion that followed, I was asked about our financial policy at Findhorn. At that time we were still living on Unemployment Benefit and considered ourselves lucky if we had a penny left by the end of the week. Our financial *policy?* For a moment I was stumped, but then found myself saying, "Well, it's quite simple. One gives up everything to put God and his will first, and then all one's needs are met from God's abundant supply." At that, many people wrote Findhorn off as "airy-fairy" and unrealistic. It was, in fact, almost three years before Sir George came to Findhorn and saw for himself that this principle really did work.

Following his visit he wrote an enthusiastic memorandum to Lady Eve Balfour, founder of the Soil Association, a group dedicated to organic farming and gardening. Sir George was sure she would be interested in our work, especially since she is the author of *The Living Soil,* a widely read book that deals with the oneness of all life and man's responsibility to the creatures he shares Earth with—animals, plants and insects. Sir George's memorandum began:

"At my Easter visit we sat on a lawn among daffodils and narcissi as beautiful and large as I have ever seen, growing in beds crowded with other flowers. I was fed on the best vegetables I have ever tasted. A young chestnut tree eight feet high stood as a central focus feature, bursting with astonishing power and vigour. Fruit trees of all sorts were in blossom—in short, one of the most vigorous and productive small gardens I have ever seen, with a quality of taste and colour unsurpassed.

"I make no claim to be a gardener, but I am a

member of the Soil Association and interested in the organic methods and have seen enough to know that compost and straw mulch alone mixed with poor and sandy soil is not enough to account for the garden. There must be, I thought, a 'Factor X' to be taken into consideration. What was it?"

After his tour around the garden Sir George was not going to accept our radio broadcast "compost and hard work" story.

"I pressed Peter Caddy for his explanation. Here we have to take the plunge and what follows will appeal to some and be unacceptable to others."

I told Sir George that "Factor X" was our cooperation with the devas and nature spirits. And he accepted it.

"The ancients, of course, accepted the kingdom of nature spirits without question as a fact of direct vision and experience. The organs of perception of the super-sensible world have atrophied in modern man as part of the price to be paid for the evolving of the analytical scientific mind. The nature spirits may be just as real as they ever were, though not to be perceived except by those who can redevelop the faculty to see and experience them. Perhaps the phenomenon with which we are now concerned is simply one of many examples of a break-through from higher planes leading to new possibilities of creative cooperation."

Not only had Sir George accepted it, but he encouraged us to write about it, thus initiating the first edition of *"The Findhorn Garden,"* a series of four booklets printed on our own hand-cranked machine. The memo Sir George had written to Lady Eve became the foreword:

"As I see it, the implications are vast. The picture the devas give is that from their viewpoint the world situation is critical. The world of nature spirits is sick of the way man is treating the life forces. The devas and elementals are working with God's law in plant growth. Man is continually violating it. There is real likelihood that they may even turn their back on man whom they sometimes consider to be a parasite on Earth. This could mean a withdrawal of life force from the plant forms, with obviously devastating results.

"Yet their wish is to work in cooperation with man, who has been given a divine task of tending the Earth. For generations man has ignored them and even denied their existence. Now a group of individuals consciously invite them into their garden. They are literally demonstrating that the desert can blossom as the rose. They also show

the astonishing pace at which this can be brought about. If this can be done so quickly at Findhorn, it can be done in the Sahara. If enough men could really begin to use this cooperation consciously, food could be grown in quantity on the most infertile areas.

"If Caddy's group have done it, many others can do so too. Wherever we are, we can invoke our devas, who doubtless are instantly in touch with those on the same wavelength anywhere else. This means that many gardeners can link up for help with centres like Findhorn where the break-through is conscious.

"The contact will not necessarily bring a scientific knowledge, though this may follow. It will work in the immediate intuition of the gardener so that his hunches may guide him to the right, though perhaps unorthodox, action. This is well demonstrated in Caddy's case, and many others who will acknowledge and love the nature spirits may, even if they are in no way sensitive, find that their gardens begin to grow and respond as never before and that they are led with surer intuition to do the right thing in planting and tending.

"The possibility of cooperation with the devas should be investigated seriously. The time has come when this can be spoken of more openly. The phenomenon of a group of amateurs doing this forces it into our attention. Many people are now ready to understand, and that enough should understand and act on it is possibly of critical importance in the present world situation."

Judging by the response we received to these booklets, there was an increasing number of people "ready to understand." They sent letters thanking us for speaking openly about our work with the devas and nature spirits and telling us how this confirmed their own experiences. Some responded out of interest in organic gardening, others related to the implications our experiments held for healing the planet, others to the spiritual aspects of our work. Findhorn was emerging into a public role.

During Sir George's visit, we were in the process of planting nearly 600 beech trees as a hedge to

enclose the area on which six new cedarwood bungalows had been erected. Our grounds now extended over nearly two acres. Paths were made through the sand, gravel and couch grass

surrounding the bungalows. We planned to prepare this area and plant it with trees, shrubs and flowers. Although our soil was considered unsuitable for deciduous trees, Pan had promised his help and that of his subjects should we decide to grow them. Eileen had received in guidance that trees draw power down from the heavens and up from the earth and that we should grow a variety to attract the many different devas.

About the middle of April I saw an advertisement in a Sunday paper with a special offer of large trees, suitable for gardens, from a nursery on the south coast of England. It seemed foolish to even consider buying these, because in this country deciduous trees should be planted by the end of March. I asked Eileen to check my inner prompting in guidance and we were told to go ahead and order them.

We waited and waited, and finally they arrived at the end of May. After ten days of transport by train, they were in a pitiful condition with shriveled leaves and roots. I truly wondered why we had been guided to get them. Getting no encouragement from the various gardeners I consulted, we went ahead and planted them in almost pure sand and in the teeth of a strong cold northeast wind. Roc was here at the time, and for several consecutive days he and Dorothy blessed the new trees, and all of us consciously gave them love and support. When Dorothy contacted the Landscape Angel for help, she was told: *We are including all these new trees and shrubs in a solid downpour of radiations, a wall of it, for they must indeed be stabilized and kept immersed in the life elements. They have to be kept in this wall without a moment's deviation; each one must be upheld until the life in them is one with it.*

Give all your protective love to this wall, and let us thank God together.

Roc invoked the aid of the nature spirits who work with this energy from the devas. He could see gnomes and elves busy at work, particularly

among the roots. The trees and shrubs survived and flourished. It seems we were guided to get them to show us that a seemingly impossible situation was possible with the help of the devas and nature spirits working through dedicated channels.

Roc's work with the nature spirits also pointed out to us the importance of the wild garden. In Britain, where there is a tradition of fine gardens, almost invariably an area in each is left wild. There is also a folk custom among farmers of leaving a bit of land, where humans are forbidden to go, as the domain of the fairies and elves.

One Sunday afternoon, Roc had accompanied a group of us on a visit to a local walled garden. At one end of the landscaped area ran a stream with a wooden bridge across it. On the other side was a wild place, cool and dense in contrast to the neat and colorful beds on our side. Roc, obeying an impulse, wandered off across the bridge and into the foliage. Later he told us that beyond a certain point in the area he had suddenly felt like an intruder. There Pan appeared beside him and told him that this part of the garden was for his subjects alone and was to be so respected. He said that in any garden, no matter the size, where the full cooperation of the nature spirits is desired a part should be left where, as far as possible, man does not enter. The nature spirits use this place as a focal point for their activity, a center from which to work.

Pan also told him that at Findhorn we did not have enough respect for our wild garden. Indeed, we had developed the habit of crossing this area when we went to the beach for a swim, and right in the middle of it Dennis had set up his tent. You can imagine how quickly he removed both himself and his gear on hearing this message! Thereafter, we made sure to enter this area as seldom as possible.

Throughout 1968 the gardens surrounding the bungalows grew. So did the number of horticultural experts we attracted. Lady Eve Balfour had found Sir George's memorandum fascinating and passed it on to her sister, Lady Mary, who came that autumn to visit. Although she modestly describes herself as "an ordinary gardener of the organic school," Lady Mary has a store of knowledge acquired through many years of study and collaboration with her sister in agricultural research experiments carried out on their farm. As we walked about the gardens together, despite her desire to rationally explain away what she saw, she was thoroughly impressed and, as she wrote, "I stared in a kind of rapturous wonder at the compact mass

of colour and form." Her report goes on to say: "The impression uppermost in my mind is that something important is happening here at Findhorn—something strange and wonderful, hopefully not unique. Gardens like this are needed the world over, desperately needed where deserts flourish and life dies. Life! Perhaps that's it! Yes, if I were asked to describe the Findhorn garden in one word, I would answer 'life.' Life abounding."

On Lady Eve's recommendation, Professor R. Lindsay Robb, consultant to the Soil Association, arrived in early 1969. With a background in agriculture, conservation and nutrition, Professor Robb had served as a consultant in various posts around the world, including the United Nations mission to Costa Rica. He clearly was a man with the wisdom as well as the knowledge of the land. As Lady Eve wrote of him, he expressed "not only love for, but a profound understanding of all forms of life, from human beings and what makes them tick, to the myriad microscopic beings whose home is the soil."

Roc and I took Lindsay around the garden. He kept picking up the powdery soil, looking at the partially broken down compost on it and exclaiming in amazement that things shouldn't be growing here at all. After his tour, he wrote: "The vigour, health and bloom of the plants in this garden at midwinter on land which is almost barren powdery sand cannot be explained by the moderate dressings of compost, nor indeed by the application of any known cultural methods of organic husbandry. There are other factors and they are vital ones.

"Living as this group is living, on the land, by the land and for the love of the land, is the practical expression of a philosophy which could be the supreme form of wisdom—and freedom."

When Lindsay Robb left, he sent up his friend and colleague, Donald Wilson, founder-secretary of the Soil Association, manager of an organic foods distribution center in London and an expert on compost.

Donald was amazed by the quality and size of our produce, but our compost, he felt, left much to be desired. He dug right in with pitchfork and hard-core technical knowledge, backed by years of Soil Association research. His two-week visit left us with our first thirty-five-ton compost heap.

Our association with him pointed out how Findhorn's knowledge could be blended with established organic gardening techniques for mutual enrichment. Donald showed us the techniques, and the devas through Dorothy answered questions he had pondered for years.

Before leaving, he put in a special request to the devas to get the new compost heap steaming. A few days later the Landscape Angel told us: *Yes, we have already begun working on the compost heap in response to Donald's request. Rejoice, a great new surge forward can be taken with the garden as the wholeness of life is more and more recognized and you work on the positive side and not through the negative way of destroying. Give many thanks, as we do.*

Donald's emphasis on creating healthy soil abundant in life, rather than concentrating on what should be done about pests and disease, supported what we had several years before received from the devas and gave us all a fresh look at how we were putting this knowledge into practice. With all visitors coming to Findhorn there was this kind of give and take: our technical knowledge was broadened, their spiritual horizons were extended.

To some we represented the fulfillment of a vision. Richard St. Barbe Baker, founder of the Society of the Men of the Trees, paid us a visit to find that his "dream for a caravan community has already been realized. It is indeed an oasis in what was once an inhospitable area of sand dunes." Having dedicated himself for over fifty years to active cooperation between man and nature to reclaim the deserts of the world through planting trees, St. Barbe saw in our gardens a living promise of success for his work.

St. Barbe Baker is one of the most dedicated and untiring people I have ever met. Nothing seems to stop him: among other accomplishments, he

initiated the Forestry Commission in Britain while pursuing higher studies in forestry at Cambridge; brought together, in 1929, the traditionally antagonistic religious heads in Palestine to discuss the future of tree-planting in the Holy Land; drafted the plan for the Civilian Conservation Corps with Franklin D. Roosevelt; organized the countries bordering the Sahara in a cooperative effort to reclaim that vast desert. He has totally given his life to heal the Earth.

During his first visit to Findhorn, St. Barbe Baker, known, in fact, as the "Man of the Trees," drew up a complete plan for the care and landscaping of the trees in our garden. Since we were still in the process of compiling and publishing our four-part garden story, we asked him to write the foreword to the section on messages from the tree devas. He wrote: "The messages from tree devas through Dorothy reveal the occult explanation that scientific research has been unable to give. The ancients believed that the Earth itself is a sentient being and feels the behaviour of mankind upon it. I submit that we accept this and behave accordingly, and thus open up for ourselves a new world of understanding.

"How dull life would be if we did not accept anything we could not explain. Think of the miracle of sunrise and sunset in the Sahara; the miracle of growth from the tiny germinating seed to the forest giant, a veritable citadel in itself providing food and shelter for myriads of tiny things, and an indispensable link in the nature cycle, giving the breath of life to man."

The devas, of course, love St. Barbe Baker. During his visit the Leylands Cypress Deva told us: *There is high rejoicing in our kingdoms as the Man of the Trees, so beloved of us, links with you here. Is it not an example in your worlds that it is one world, one work, one cause under God being expressed through different channels?*

You understand better now why we have gone on and on about the need for trees on the surface of the Earth. Great forests must flourish and man must see to this if he wishes to continue to live on this planet. The knowledge of this necessity must become part of his consciousness; as much accepted as his need for water in order to live. He needs trees just as much; the two are interlinked. We are, indeed, the skin of the Earth, and a skin not only covers and protects, but passes through it the vital forces of life. Nothing could be more vital to life as a whole than trees.

Clearly, we found support and understanding in each other. A phrase from a prayer by Richard St. Barbe Baker adequately expresses our mutual meeting ground: *Help us give our best to life and leave the Earth a little more beautiful for having lived on it.*

The Findhorn garden had demonstrated what could be done by man working hand-in-hand with the devas and nature spirits. Now we had the acceptance and support of others with more technical knowledge. Just at this time new lessons began coming our way.

My pledge to seek cooperation and brotherhood with the nature forces was sincere, but I found it was not always easy to carry out in practice. The problem was to differentiate between the traditional gardening practices that took the devic and elemental kingdoms into account and those that simply exploited them. The decision rested squarely on my shoulders. I had been given the authority, as man, to act in the garden. Though occasionally I slipped, I was told: *As long as you make consistent steps toward change on behalf of man, mistakes in the moment will be overlooked and balanced out.* My experience in dealing with the delicate sweet peas was a perfect example of the type of challenge I had to confront.

As a child I had watched my father grow sweet peas in the traditional manner, allowing only one main stem from each plant to grow, pinching out all other stems. Flowers were permitted to bloom only when a single strong stem had grown with no tendrils or side shoots. The result was a long-stemmed sweet pea with four or five large blooms. To me this was the standard for sweet pea beauty.

Thus, when Eileen asked me to grow sweet peas for the two tall vases in the community sanctuary, I knew how to go about getting the most beautiful sweet peas possible. These were after all for the glory of God, not man. I grew these plants as I had learned, but also with much love. Each day I talked to the sweet peas, telling them how lovely they were and what magnificent sweet pea blossoms they were growing—while I pinched off their tendrils and sideshoots. Dorothy, of course, wasn't happy about this. Nor was Roc, who felt it was clearly manipulation.

This was all very frustrating and even infuriating. Gardening to me had meant pinching out, pruning, weeding, thinning and otherwise creating the conditions that would give the plants we had brought into our garden a chance to grow and be fruitful. In the natural environment of a field or forest, a bush is pruned by animals eating back the growth, and I felt that in a garden man could take the place of nature and do the same. Besides, without pruning, fruit trees and bushes can't bear fruit, and cultivated roses can't give those beautiful blossoms. That's just fact. In order to create, one must, in a sense, destroy as well. Were the nature kingdoms telling me to stop tending the garden? I just couldn't see an alternative.

Attempting to settle the controversy, Dorothy contacted the Sweet Pea Deva. She received a very straightforward message, emphasizing the *natural* beauty of the sweet pea. However, the deva presented to us a way of bringing about change in the form of plants without causing harm—through cooperation with the inner spirit of the plant, rather than manipulation of the outer form. Again we were being told to look to the creative power of our thoughts. We were told to ask the nature kingdoms, in faith, for the change we wanted to initiate. Then, if our faith was strong enough and the change was clearly for the good of the whole, they would cooperate to bring it about.

However, the devas had said that we were just beginning to move into a new era of cooperation. In our garden, we were in the interim period of building a bridge to that new world. Therefore, I had to follow my inner feeling that it would not be right to suddenly drop all traditional gardening practices. This would lead to chaos. One builds the new by taking the best of the old and adding onto it. Moreover, we often did not have enough people or time—or indeed the necessary level of consciousness—to do more than keep the garden well-tended. That was a big enough job in itself.

Over and over we were reminded that in this garden of cooperation our aim is to work with the nature kingdoms in a balanced way, discovering plant forms that are expressive of both man and nature. As Lady Eve Balfour, in a letter to me, wrote: "Just as we have to learn to be aware that we *occupy* a physical form, so must we become aware that this is true of every life form. While we identify entities (plant, animal or man) with their forms, we will only be able to see God as divided against himself. But when we manage to reach communion with the reality behind the manifestation, we can, in cooperation, work out compromises for the forms, acceptable to all."

Perhaps, as part of this process, man must change his concept of beauty. But we must remember that the nature kingdom is evolving as well and is ready and willing to change, providing man's motive is in accord with the whole.

In 1970 a young man, David Spangler, and his spiritual colleague Myrtle Glines came to Findhorn from America. For several years before that, David had been a lecturer and writer on New Age themes. When he arrived he found us to be a dozen or so people working in a garden and living a God-centered life. Within the following eighteen months community membership grew to 150. During David's three-year stay our identity expanded into that of a New Age community and training center. His particular contacts with higher beings and his ability to clarify Findhorn's broader role helped to bring this about. The intense energy I had directed toward initiating and developing the garden now began to shift into administrative areas. While I remained responsible to the vision of cooperation, the actual physical work in the garden had been taken over by other members. Findhorn's focus now was the flowering of human consciousness. The lessons we had learned growing plants we now applied to growing the people who joined us.

Our work in the garden had deeply rooted the energies of love and light in the very soil of Findhorn. The forces of nature had been our teachers, providing us with physical and spiritual nourishment. Just as in the evolution of the planet, plants had provided the environment that made it possible for man to develop, each of the plants we had been guided to grow here contributed its energies toward creating the proper environment for Findhorn's greater work: the transformation of the human soul.

Indeed, the growth of the garden is symbolic of the growth of the soul. The proper environment must be created, weeds that might choke out the finer, more delicate qualities of the soul must be removed, and all actions must be guided by the love that fulfills all laws. Just as you can create conditions for insuring the growth of plants, so the quality of life within the Findhorn community can be likened to a greenhouse environment where the growth and transformation of each individual is stepped up.

In the beginning, while we were in the midst of establishing the garden, we could not see what it was moving toward. Thus, we had to live in the moment with faith in God's guidance. Now, looking back, a clear pattern and plan can be discerned, each apparent challenge seen as teaching the perfect lesson. A man quite untutored in the techniques of gardening was placed in this unpromising terrain and challenged to create a garden. He was provided with all the necessary channels and situations necessary to revive in him the spirit of true cooperation with nature, under the guidance of the God within. And the garden grew.

Much has been demonstrated at Findhorn of what can be done in a spirit of cooperation between man and nature. There is so much we have yet to do. In the new phase of experimentation we are moving into in the garden, we must begin to live more fully what we have been given. Some of the directives we have received present great challenges, but we know we must proceed as we have always done, step-by-step, in faith that we are revealing the oneness of all life.

You can liken what you are doing to what Noah did under My minute instructions. I gave him every detail word by word, and he followed it out without hesitation. He did question as you question, but once I had explained the situation he went steadily on, following out My instructions. And the impossible was brought about: the ark rose in water as I said it would.

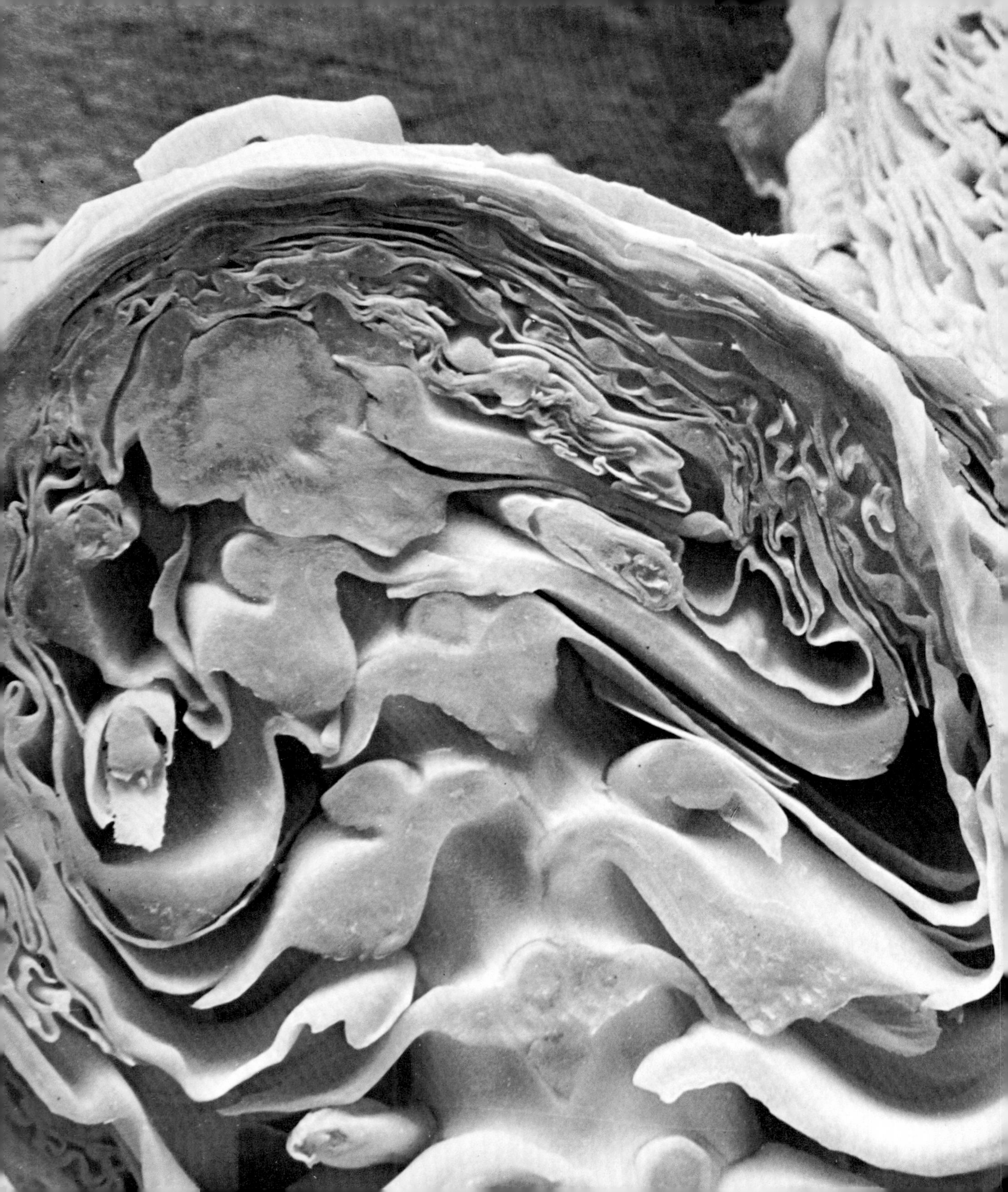

Your way is true and simple,
the way it was in the beginning
when man and I walked hand in hand,
talking to one another.

EILEEN

THE KINGDOM OF LIGHT. I do not claim to understand many of the things that happened to us during the growth of the garden and of the Findhorn community. Nor do I have any particular advice to give, except that the most important thing is for each individual to look within for his or her own answers. Perhaps if I share with you some of our experiences, you will see how every aspect of our lives was guided by this turning within.

Living in such close quarters for seven years, we certainly learned a great deal. Our three boys, born one year apart, were just beginning primary school, and you know what boys are like. When they came home from school they used to bring all their friends and play in the living room, so there really was nowhere to sit. Peter spent most of his time in the garden, Dorothy had the annex, and my special place was the kitchen. This was

built along the passageway between the boys' tiny room and the sitting room which also served as a bedroom for Peter and myself, and at mealtimes, as a dining room.

In the evening, after the boys had gone to bed, Dorothy, Peter and I could move into the living room to read or watch television. We also meditated there together each night. The children had grown up with this and knew we needed quiet. To them, our meditation was natural. In fact, I remember the way Christopher used to tell me to turn to God when I was in doubt about something. "God will know the answer, Mum," he would say with such confidence. And I would think, *Out of the mouths of babes . . . .*

It was a good situation in which to learn self-discipline. Peter, Dorothy and I were such strong individuals, yet we had to learn how to work together as a group. *You have to learn to work together perfectly like fingers on a hand,* my guidance had told us. *You are all individuals very specially chosen and trained by Me to do a specific work which only you can do.* Yet no matter how different our tasks and approaches were, the one thing we were all learning was to see everything with new eyes. This is how we could create the new all around us. *As you go about your everyday tasks today, try to see each one in a new light. Do them as if you have never done them before, as if each action is new and wonderful and exciting. Let life be like that to you and you will find your whole outlook will change. You will indeed love what you are doing because you are doing it for Me and with Me.*

Always it was our attitude that was most important. What we were thinking was reflected in our everyday lives. If we looked at a situation negatively, it became negative. But if we made that extra effort, which was often very hard to do, we could truly make a situation new.

The little things provided the real tests. For instance, I preferred cooking or gardening to doing the housework. So for me the real challenge was to enjoy cleaning the caravan, wholeheartedly and therefore perfectly. I was told that in something like polishing the floor, *You can do it positively so you really enjoy seeing a lovely shine come up as you rub, or you can do it negatively and just feel it is another job that must be done. When you start on a job, whatever it may be, see that your attitude towards it is right, and how very different it will be. Your attitude makes it one thing or another.*

Everything we were doing in our daily living—working in the garden, eating the food from it, absorbing the sunshine and fresh air—was teaching us to live in a new way, with joy in every moment and deep sensitivity to all things around us. We could see that each of us by our thoughts and actions could lift our spirits and surroundings. We couldn't create a new world without being new ourselves, and we had to work constantly at keeping our spirits high. *Whenever you feel you need a break, take a walk and enjoy the wonders of nature all around you. If you open your eyes you cannot fail to see them. All of that helps to keep your vibrations raised.*

When I look back I see that, despite all the challenges of our situation, it was actually a very happy time—perhaps the happiest time of all—because our lives were so simple. My guidance at that time told us, *Life is not really complicated. In fact, it is very simple. It is simplicity itself, but you make it complicated. When you find life is getting to be too much for you and you feel weighed down, stop and look at a child. A child lives fully in the moment, enjoying what he is doing. He does not worry about tomorrow and what it might bring. That is how you should live. Be ever conscious of the wonder of life.*

Yes, we were like children then, and God was still somewhat like the Father, separate and above us, reaching down to help. But gradually I have come to understand what it means to find that same God within myself. I have come to see that our lives are being carefully and lovingly guided by his voice speaking within me. Listening for every whisper of it was my main role in creating the garden and the community at Findhorn.

The first time I heard this voice was in 1953, when Peter and I were visiting Glastonbury, a center of spiritual power in England. I was sitting in the stillness of a small private sanctuary there, when I heard a voice—a very clear voice—within me. I had never experienced anything like that before. It simply said, *Be still and know that I am God.* What is this? I thought. Am I going mad? I had been brought up in the Church of England and learned in Sunday school about the "still small voice within"—but when you actually *hear* a voice, it's a different matter. I was really quite shocked, because it was so clear.

I don't want to give the idea that this just happened, without any preparation. There had been a great deal of spiritual training leading up to that point. Yet hearing this voice was totally unexpected. Following the experience, I went through a painful period of conflict and tension when I kept hearing many different voices, all battling to be first. I just kept listening and listening until I heard one clear voice again, and then all the others disappeared.

What greater or more wonderful relationship could man ask for than the knowledge that he is truly one with Me, that I am in you and you are in Me. Accepting the reality of this oneness came slowly. In fact, at first I felt it was audacious even to speak of such a thing. Yet I couldn't deny my experience. I know that God is within each one of us, within everything. I feel that the Church teaches about the God outside of us, but that's the same God as the one within. You can call him by different names if you like, but there's only one God.

Eventually receiving guidance from the voice of God became the most natural thing in the world. *Listening to My voice has become as natural to you as breathing. There is no strain about it whatsoever. It should never be necessary for you to come into a special state before you can hear My voice. You should be able to hear it at all times, in all places, no matter what is happening around you, no matter what state you may be in. Your need for Me is constant. As it was in the beginning when man walked and talked with Me, so it is now happening again. This is the relationship I long to have with all My children.*

I would never say that hearing this voice within, as I hear it, is the only way of experiencing God. It isn't, because everybody has a different way. That's just my way of doing it. God is within everyone, the very thing everyone lives by, although it is not always realized. So anybody can have closeness with him. It's just a question of whether you want it badly enough. *Do you not realize that you have within you all wisdom, all knowledge, all understanding? You do not have to seek it without, but you have to take time to be still and to go deep within to find it. Many souls are too lazy or feel that there is so much to be done that they have no time to be still and go into the silence. They prefer to live on someone else's wisdom and knowledge instead of receiving it direct from the source themselves.*

I certainly had to learn to put my communion with the God within before anything else. I had to learn to be still. I find that when my mind is wandering all over the place, nothing happens. But when I am still, in communion with the "withinness," then things really begin to happen.

When the six of us were packed into that tiny caravan, the only place I could go for complete quiet was down to the public toilets of the caravan park. I'd bundle up against the cold and sit there for two or three hours every night. It was a place where I could shut the door and have no interruptions. Ridiculous as it may seem, it was actually quite lovely. But it wasn't always easy, of course. During the day I was cooking, taking care of the children and sometimes helping in the garden. Some nights I was so tired it was an effort even to hold the pen and write down the guidance I was receiving. But I knew I had to put first things first. *The choice is not something that you do once and it becomes permanent, but all day and every day this choice lies in your hands. Every decision you make, you choose whether you make it for the small self or whether you seek My divine guidance and follow that.*

I still have a lot to learn. It's easy to get into a lovely comfortable rut, having special times for quiet and meditation, and special times for writing the guidance down and reading it out to others. But to *live* what I have received is far more difficult. I have recorded over thirty thousand pages of guidance since we came to Findhorn, and now to put it into practice, to recognize it as a true part of myself, is the challenge. Back in 1964 I was told, *The time will come in the future when you will no longer have to sit down and record everything that I have to say to you. You will learn to have your antennae out all the time, listening for every minute instruction as I send it forth. As Peter now has to be guided in action, so*

will all of you have to do the same. My word will mean action.

Actually, it was Peter who helped me to accept my guidance as truth. All along he had faith that I was hearing God's voice, and whenever I had doubts or fears, he would encourage me. Without his help, I feel neither Dorothy nor I would have developed our contacts with other realms. Peter was constantly after us, encouraging us to make these contacts, then acting on what we received. At the time we felt he was pushing us, and we didn't, in fact, feel very grateful. We used to get quite annoyed. But the point eventually came when I felt that this deep inner contact with the God within was the one thing I wanted more than anything else. Besides, following guidance proved to be the most practical way to live. We were told, *Put My messages to the test and see for yourself whether they are of the truth, until you know without a shadow of a doubt that they are and that they work when you live them.* As I saw that what I received within was actually materializing around us, my faith grew.

However, I didn't understand many of the things I received in guidance at the time. For example, in early 1964 we were told, *Peter is in the garden to plant and produce high vibrational foodstuffs to be eaten by all of you to help raise your vibrations and create a light body.* Now, what on earth was a light body? I hadn't a clue, and we were in such isolation that we had no idea whether other spiritual groups were going through the same thing. Our only reference was within us, as guidance said. *What I have told you about the diet I want you to follow has nothing to do with any known or written diet. This is something new. Therefore, if at any time you have a query about it, ask Me for the answer; you will not find it in a book. You are pioneering for Me, therefore follow out My instructions step-by-step.*

The instructions were explicit. *You can eat butter and cheese in abundance. The salads you eat are good. Take more olive oil. Not so many potatoes are necessary, but eat as much as you like of fresh vegetables. It is alright to eat fish, but twice a week is enough. Eggs you can eat in abundance, cooked any way you wish. It is not right to eat a lot of cakes and scones, but once in a while it is alright.*

Since our hotel days we had been gradually

reducing the amount of meat we were eating. First we had cut out red meat, then white, then poultry. This took about a year altogether, and we had a lot of other habits to break, as well. Peter had, in fact, been trained in catering and so had gourmet tastes. Besides, he was working so hard in the garden that it seemed he would need meat protein, but I received, *Tell Peter to eat more honey. It will give him plenty of energy. You will find that then he doesn't need so much protein. Tell him to try this even if it means he will have to come and get a spoonful every now and again.*

We began to realize that everything our bodies were absorbing during this time was of vital importance. That is why we had to eat the produce from our own garden. No artificial fertilizers or insecticides were being used, devas and nature spirits were tending the garden, and all of us were contributing our positive thoughts and vibrations to the plants. *I want you to realize that the produce out of this garden will do you more good than anything bought. It has tremendous life force in it, which is the main thing that you need. This food is blessed by Me.*

We developed an entirely new understanding of the purpose of eating. We were told that we were purifying the atomic structure of our bodies, transforming the dense physical substance into light and lightness which would be more receptive to absorbing energies from the sun, sea and air, and

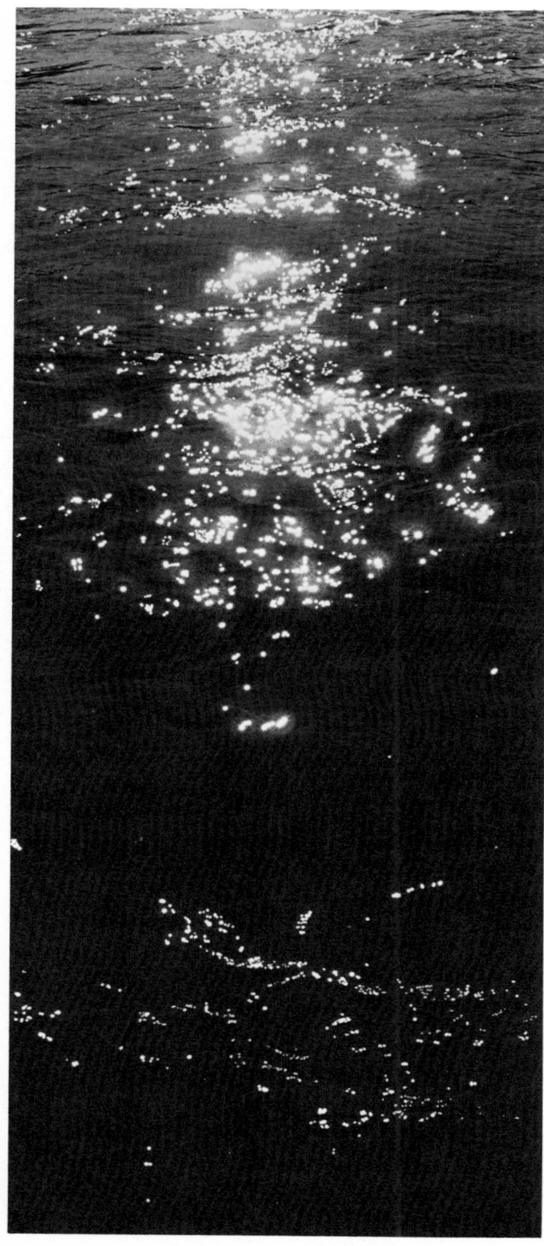

would require less solid food. But this was not a process that could be rushed into. *You have to gradually refine your body. As it becomes finer and less dense, your skin will begin to be able to absorb substances which at present it is incapable of doing. It is as if layer after layer of old skin has to be peeled off, leaving only the fine thin layer which can absorb these purities from the ethers. I ask all of you to drink more water, just pure, pure water. It is very cleansing and will be a great help in speeding up this refining process.*

Previously we had thought of food in terms of calories or energy needed for building and maintaining solid physical bodies. Now we were told that what actually nourished us was a more subtle energy. Through our diet we were absorbing the light that made the vegetables and fruits grow—the light of the sun and the light of our consciousness. Our bodies were becoming light.

Pure clear water was vital to this process of transforming our bodies. Over and over we were told to drink little else. *You do not need tea for tea stimulates and is unnecessary and harmful for what you are doing at this time. It would be better to drink milk if you really feel you need it, otherwise water. Coffee should not be taken; your system does not need it.* What we did need was the effect of water's special qualities. *Water has untapped forces and energies in it which have not yet been discovered by mankind. Sunshine and water, sunshine and water. I want you to cut down gradually on solid food and drink more water. Do it for My sake, because I have asked you to and for no other reason. Water will give you the energy you need.*

I didn't really understand all this, but I listened

and wrote down what I heard. *There are tremendous forces being released on the planet at this time. Forces which are being energized by water. Like the genie in the bottle, they at last have been freed. Water is the medium which is to be used to energize these forces. Water on the body. Water in the body. Water all around you. That is one reason why you are living surrounded by water on three sides.*

I did become more deeply aware of water—the feeling of rain on my face, the tingling sensation, like electricity, as I put my hands in water.

Still, we didn't understand exactly why we were being asked to transform our bodies. When I asked for clarity on this, I received, *My beloved child, when you really believe with your whole heart and at all times, that man was made in My image and likeness, you will have found the greatest secret of life. Try to understand this question of a light body and dense body, to understand about the physical and the spirit body.*

I certainly knew that God wasn't saying he had a physical body like ours. Because of my upbringing, I had thought that the body was like a shell to be worn for a short time and cast off, and that the spirit alone was like God. But it seemed that this was saying something different. *Man was made in My image and likeness, then he abused his body so much by eating the wrong food, by drinking the wrong drinks, by thinking the wrong thoughts.*

What did food and drink have to do with the image and likeness of God? I can't say I understood any of this then, and I'm only beginning to come to terms with it now. Perhaps the body is to be seen not just as a temple to *contain* God, but every cell is light, is spirit, which reflects God. That's why caring properly for the body is so important.

As part of this process of refinement, we were reminded of the power and importance of our thoughts. Through them we could transform our bodies. *Always remember, you are what you think you are. Again I say to you, you must be ever conscious of these things. Never allow yourself to imagine that your body will become a light body without your doing anything about it. All the time think about building a light body, and let your thoughts help to create it.*

Before eating we always gave thanks for our food. We had been told, *Your attitude when you eat anything should be one of joy and pleasure and thanksgiving. You are to be constantly aware that all these gifts are Mine.* But it seems we have to learn to say thank you because we so often forget. Yet everything is a gift. I try to begin in the morning when I first wake up by saying thank you for the night's sleep. My guidance also told us that we should show our appreciation to the devas for their work, not only by enjoying our food but also by walking around the garden and being grateful for what we see there.

We did truly appreciate this delicious and special food from the garden, and we knew how good it was for us. But, quite honestly, I sometimes got awfully tired of salads and vegetables. For about eight years, we were living almost completely on our own produce. At one point, just when we really needed it, I received, *It is so important that you really enjoy what you are eating and not do it out of a sense of duty. You get tired of eating salads day after day and instead of doing something about it, you just struggle on. It is so important that you learn to go with whatever you are doing and give of yourself a hundred per cent. It would do you far more good to sit down and eat a handful of raisins and nuts or whatever you really fancy instead of sitting there, pushing down salad because everyone else is doing it and you have been told that it is good for you. Next time you feel this way about the food you are eating, stop and have something different. It will change your whole attitude. I say this to all of you. Don't be like a lot of sheep.*

Strain and resistance could not possibly lift our bodies or spirits. That was one of the reasons why Peter had been guided to grow that enormous range of fruits and vegetables—so that we could have variety and joy in our diet. Every day for our midday meal we had huge salads, sometimes using up to twenty different vegetables and herbs. It seemed like mountains of salad, and I used to wonder how Peter could get through it all. Eventually though, we did find that the life-filled food from our garden was so nourishing that we needed to eat far less than we had been used to.

The children had their lunch at school, so it was only their evening meal that was vegetarian. Children find it difficult to eat salads all the time, so I used to stew garden vegetables with dumplings or make a dish like cauliflower-cheese. They liked their mum's cooking anyway, so that was fine!

Preparing food from our own garden held such a deep and simple pleasure. When I was aware in the moment of what I was doing, just going out into the garden to pick the vegetables for a meal became a joyful task. I had received in guidance, *It is good to prepare vegetables with real appreciation for what you are doing, thus enabling the radiations of light to enter the food. A potato is no longer just a potato in your hands, but a thing of real beauty. You can feel it is something living, vibrating. Just stop and think what a difference this makes to the vegetables. Sometimes you feel your heart will burst with joy and appreciation.*

As I took each pea pod or bean from the plant, I could see how alive everything was. I could feel each one of those vegetables as a living being in my hands. Of course, I would never have got the meals made if I had been constantly stopping to consider each vegetable. But every now and again, I got guidance about it, or I was suddenly struck by the wonder of nature and of what I was doing, and I would think, How amazing life is!

Living right in the midst of the garden made us see how much our lives and the lives of the vegetables were connected. They were our main diet, and we returned all our waste to them through the compost. Thus the oneness of life was an everyday experience as we watched the cycle complete itself, from the plants to us and back again.

After gathering the vegetables, I would wash and cut them outdoors on the patio when the weather was fine. It was lovely to sit there, absorbing the sun, breathing fresh air and preparing something like carrots or radishes that only a few minutes before had been growing in the earth. What a wonder that they had come from tiny seeds and now were so large and vibrant. *When you make a salad, as you handle each vegetable or herb, let your mind dwell on how each was made. You can feel the struggle that some of them have had to pull through, whereas with others, you can feel the ease and freedom in which they have been brought to fruition. All these thoughts and feelings are important. They bring the very life force into your body.*

Eating this way certainly did make us more sensitive. In our isolated circumstances, that was fine. But as more and more people came to visit us or to join the community, our diet had to be modified so as not to separate ourselves. Anyway, the guidance we had received related to our own needs at a specific time, so I certainly couldn't expect others to follow it.

I feel it is far more important for each individual to go within and find out what is best for his or her own self. That is why I prefer not to call myself an authority on anything. When you are an "authority," you place yourself above others. When you know

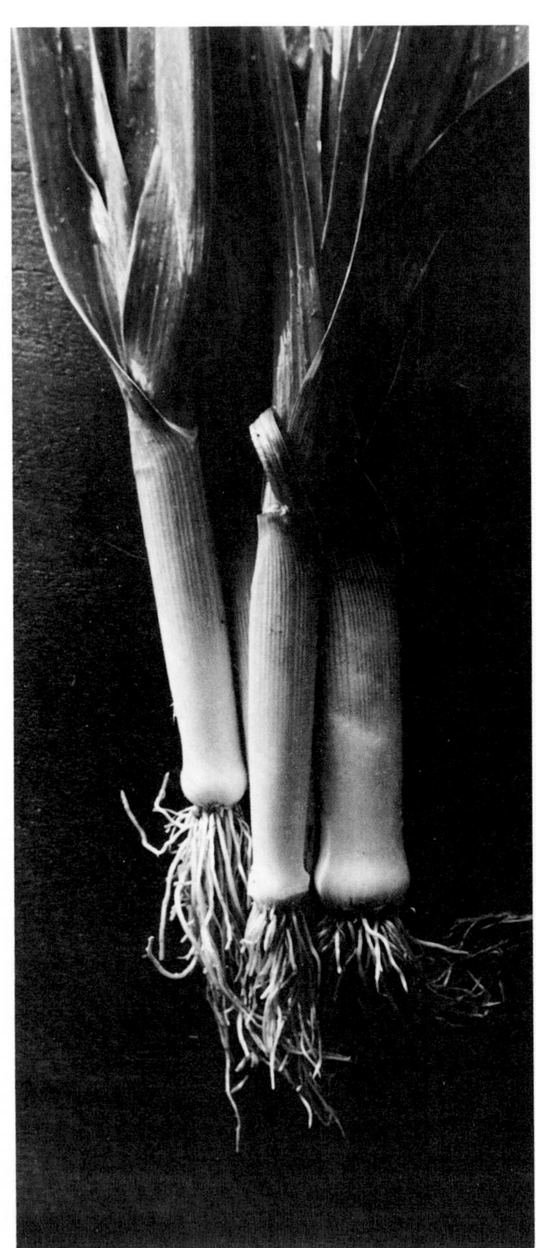

you are not, then you are on the same level and you can talk, person to person. You can communicate. So it's just practical. To me, the only true authority is the voice of God within each individual, in whatever way that may express itself.

Therefore, whatever you eat, I feel, is up to you. I think you can eat just about anything, because it is not the actual food that one takes in that is most important but the *attitude,* the love, with which you prepare and eat it. Even while we were going through that refining process, it was stressed that our thoughts had as much effect as the food we were taking in. So now, for instance, when we are away from Findhorn, which still basically serves vegetarian food, and someone offers me something that I usually don't eat, like roast beef and Yorkshire pudding, I don't say to my hostess, "I'm sorry, but I can't eat that." What I do is encircle the food with love, I bless it, then I eat it and enjoy it.

It's so easy to develop the idea that it is wrong to eat certain kinds of food. For this very reason, one of Peter's favorite stories is about my "steak and whiskey diet." He revels in telling it, especially when he knows he's talking to a group of avid vegetarians.

The story behind it is simple enough. Several years ago I had to go into the hospital for an operation. When I returned home I found I just couldn't face salads. I had lost a lot of weight, yet was barely eating anything. All I longed for was a piece of meat. One of the community members was looking after me at the time and I kept thinking, Oh dear, what would she think? I was sure she wouldn't like to cook meat in her bungalow where I was staying. Eventually I plucked up my courage and said, "You know, Joanie, one thing I'd really love . . . is a piece of steak." "Why didn't you tell me before?" she said and went off to the butcher. I didn't eat anything else, just steak every other day. It was very extravagant. But I was so anemic and my body knew what was needed to build me up again.

The whiskey was to help me sleep at night after the operation. For years I had been in the rhythm of spending several hours each night in meditation. After surgery I was too weak to continue that rhythm, but I just couldn't get to sleep. "Oh, the best thing for you is an old-fashioned remedy—hot whiskey and lemon with a little sugar," the doctor said. "That will fix you up." And that was my "steak and whiskey" diet. Actually quite sensible and not very dramatic, but if you don't know the details it can sound shocking. "Oh yes, Eileen went on a steak and whiskey diet, you know," Peter says to these audiences. And I just wriggle in my seat, watching the horror spread across their faces.

During those early years, our lives and the life of the garden were inseparable. Peter, of course, was spending most of his time either reading about gardening or actually doing it. Each of us contributed in some way. Dorothy and I used to drive down to Findhorn Bay, while the boys were in school, and collect seaweed off the rocks. Our hands used to

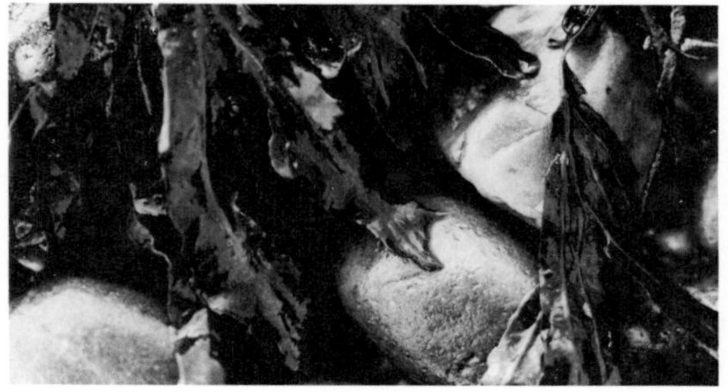

get absolutely blue with the cold, but it was necessary to get this seaweed for the compost. Sometimes there happened to be a dead salmon or swan lying on the beach and we would add that to our collection and, holding our noses, bring it along with us. We collected anything organic along the shore that seemed good for compost. We were very compost-minded!

I really enjoyed working in the garden. I have always loved flowers and other plants. As a child I spent a good deal of time on my grandmother's farm in Ireland, and I have a love for the soil itself. So I could really understand what it meant when guidance told me, *It is necessary to work with the soil, to love the soil and feel it alive in your hands. When it is not alive, bring it to life with love and tenderness, with care and feeling. All this brings you closer to the things that really matter in life.* We were told that each of us had a particular kind of radiation to give to the soil and the garden. Quite honestly, I hadn't a clue what radiations were. It didn't mean a thing to me, but this is what kept on coming in guidance. We were told that it was frightfully important, *not only for now in what you are doing for this garden, but it is for the reconstruction of this earth.* So I would go out into the garden to work, trying to keep in mind that I was putting radiations into the soil and plants. Then one day while I was spreading compost I became totally concentrated on what I was doing and I could actually feel the life force flowing through me. I *knew* that I was doing more than helping the plants and soil just physically. As the months went by, my heart overflowed with gratitude to see the area around our caravan coming alive through all the work Peter and the rest of us were doing with the assistance of the nature forces.

Peter was the one who had the vision for the garden, and he would tell us what needed to be done. Sometimes I rather resented that, because I would get out into the garden and see a certain path that needed weeding, for instance, and think, Oh, I would like to work right along there today. Then Peter would come along and say, "There is compost that needs to be put out," or "That area needs to be watered." At times like that, I had to start loving what I was doing, no matter what it was.

Sometimes all of us, including the children, worked in the garden together. When Peter began leveling the slope at the back of the caravan and found it was just stones and gravel, we got our children and their friends from round about the caravan site and collected these stones in buckets to be hauled away. Of course, we had to inspire them and make it like a game, but it was working together, and that was fun.

Sometimes we took sacks into the woods to collect leaves and grass for the compost. And then in the autumn there was always blackberry picking. We would pile into the car and drive around the countryside looking for a good place to pick berries for jam and jelly. The children loved that. They'd come back with their hands and faces absolutely black. They always ate as much as they wanted—usually more than they managed to gather.

We never forced them to do any work in the garden if they didn't want to, however. In fact we never forced anything on them. We just let them know they had a part to play and encouraged a sense of responsibility. We were gardeners for the children as well, helping their spirits to grow and blossom. *Tend My special flowers with very special*

care, my guidance had told us. *Flowers unfold slowly and gently, bit by bit in the sunshine, and a soul, too, must never be pushed or driven but unfolds in its own perfect timing to reveal its true wonder and beauty.* By keeping a positive attitude toward them we could bring out the best in each. When we saw in them, for example, the desire to "get" give way to the desire to "give," without any direct suggestion from us, my heart was filled with gratitude. We knew that it came from within them and therefore was true. *It comes from Me, the spirit of all good which is in the center of every soul.*

It is the role of Findhorn now to nurture this spirit in all those who come in contact with us. Our work is to be gardeners of souls, wherever we are. *The seeds are beginning to germinate. Tend them with the greatest care. Never trample on them and ignore them. They are very tender and very delicate. Water them with love. Let the light of My truth shine upon them gently to begin with, gradually becoming stronger as they become stronger. Be good gardeners and bring forth good and perfect fruit.*

The devas, who at first seemed to be far-off beings,
through a joyous communion grew into close companions
until eventually they made me realize
that they, like the kingdom of heaven, are within.

THE DEVA CONSCIOUSNESS. My contact with the devas opened up in a natural way, rising organically from my life background. My two brothers and I were brought up by the most delightful and loving parents in a beautiful old house next to a wood in Canada. We had gardens of vegetables and flowers, but I was not especially attracted to cultivated plants. I loved wandering in the wild places.

I went to university with a lot of questions, but despite all the talk about the profundities of life, I found no satisfactory answers. Eventually I started paying attention to that voice within that had long been asking me to listen, and I began to write down the daily guidance I was receiving. During a period of spiritual training which was teaching me to place the will of this indwelling God first in my life, I met Peter and Eileen Caddy. Before moving to Findhorn, we worked together on the staff of the hotel where Peter was manager, putting this principle into action.

When I speak of God's will, I am aware that this might call up a stereotyped picture of an old gentleman somewhere out in the sky, making automatons of us by imposing an external will. This is not my meaning, but I do not know of another way in which to convey it. To me, God is an indwelling presence, the core of what I am and what everything is. God is life itself, speaking through all life. And God's will is the path we tread which develops the best for us and for all we encounter. *Let My will be a mystery for you to find in each moment,* my guidance told me. *Seek it within the little and the big. It includes all people and all things, all questions and all answers.*

Our first winter at Findhorn had been an especially harsh one for the area, with frequent gale-force winds adding to the snow and rain. But by early May, 1963, the first radishes and lettuce Peter had sown in the patio garden were coming up, and he was busy preparing another area for peas and beans and a few other vegetables. The spring weather was growing warm enough for us to sit outside on the patio during our daily time of quiet together. This was a delightful opportunity to experience God's presence in everything around me.

During that period of time, my guidance had been telling me to be open for new ideas and inspiration: *Be prepared, My child, and on the lookout for My promptings. Expect new ideas to come into your head. This is a further period of training for you and it entails many new things.* The guidance I received on the morning of May 8 was indeed the beginning of something new: *One of the jobs for you as My free child is to feel into the nature forces, such as the wind. Feel its essence and purpose for Me, and be positive and harmonize with that essence. It will not be as difficult as you immediately imagine because the beings of these forces will be glad to feel a friendly power. All forces are to be felt into, even the sun, the moon, the sea, the trees, the very grass. All are part of My life. All is one life. Play your part in making life one again, with My help.*

Well, I thought that was very nice, because as far as I was concerned, there was nothing I would like better than to sit in the sun and commune with nature. But when Peter saw this guidance, that's

not how he understood it. "You can use that to help with the garden!" he said, feeling that direct contact with the nature forces might give him the answers he needed to his questions about the garden. Sure enough, the next day I was told in guidance, *Yes, you are to cooperate in the garden. Begin this by thinking about the nature spirits, the higher over lighting nature spirits, and tune into them. That will be so unusual as to draw their interest here. They will be overjoyed to find some members of the human race eager for their help. That is the first step.*

By the higher nature spirits, I mean those such as the spirits of clouds, of rain, and of vegetables. The smaller individual nature spirits are under their jurisdiction. In the new world these realms will be quite open to humans—or I should say, humans will be open to them. Seek into the glorious realms of nature with sympathy and understanding, knowing that these beings are of the Light, willing to help, but suspicious of humans and on the look-out for the false, the snags. Keep with Me and they will find none, and you will all build towards the new.

I thought such instructions rather a tall order, taxing my credulity and certainly beyond my talents. I knew only a little about nature spirits and, although I was aware of the angelic hierarchy, I had not known that there were devas overlighting vegetables. I told Peter I couldn't do it and stalled for several weeks, despite his encouragement. However, instructions from the inner divinity—and Peter's promptings—are not lightly disregarded!

One evening in meditation I reached a powerful state of heightened consciousness, and I thought, now I'll contact one of those higher nature spirits. Since vegetables had been mentioned, I thought I might contact the spirit of some plant we were growing at Findhorn. I had always been fond of the garden pea which we had grown at home in Canada, and I could feel in sympathy in all ways with that plant. So I tried to focus on the essence of what the pea was to me and the love I felt for it. I got an immediate response in thought and feeling which I put into the following words: *I can speak to you, human. I am entirely directed by my work which is set out and molded and which I merely bring to fruition, yet you have come straight to my awareness. My work is clear before me—to bring the force fields into manifestation regardless of obstacles, and there are many in this man-infested world. While the vegetable kingdom holds no grudge against those it feeds, man takes what he can as a matter of course, giving no thanks. This makes us strangely hostile.*

What I would tell you is that as we forge ahead, never deviating from our course for one moment's thought, feeling or action, so could you. Humans generally seem not to know where they are going or why. If they did, what a powerhouse they would be. If they were on the straight course of what is to be done, we could cooperate with them! I have put across my meaning and bid you farewell.

When I showed this to Peter, he said, "Fine, now you can find out what to do about these tomatoes and what it is these lettuces might need . . . ." And I would take his questions to the deva of the species concerned and get straightforward practical advice.

At this point I might say that the term "deva" is a Sanskrit word meaning shining one. On the whole, I have chosen to use this word rather than the English equivalent, "angel," which calls up stereotyped images that are more of a barrier than a help in understanding the true nature of these beings.

It wasn't until nearly ten years later that I was introduced to some of the esoteric literature on devas. However, through my own contact with them we discovered that they are part of a whole hierarchy of beings, from the earthiest gnome to the highest archangel, and are a sister evolution to the human on earth. The devas hold the archetypal pattern and plan for all forms around us, and they direct the energy needed for materializing them. The physical bodies of minerals, vegetables, animals and humans are all energy brought into form through the work of the devic kingdom. Sometimes we call that work natural law, but it is the devas who carry out that law, ceaselessly and joyfully. The level of this hierarchy I was guided to contact was not that of the spirit of, say, a particular pea plant in our garden, but rather the overlighting intelligence, the soul essence, of all peas throughout the world.

While the devas might be considered the "architects" of plant forms, the nature spirits or elementals, such as gnomes and fairies, may be seen

as the "craftsmen," using the blueprint and energy channeled to them by the devas to build up the plant form. It was with these beings that R. Ogilvie Crombie established communication. When Roc joined our work at Findhorn, he helped to clarify and confirm certain undefined feelings I had had about the plant world. For instance, while I could not explain why I was upset when the gorse bushes were pruned in full blossom, Roc was able to clarify exactly what was wrong through his contact with the nature spirits.

Essentially, the devas are energy, they are life force. (We humans are as well, only in our own unique way.) I was told in guidance, *You are simply surrounded by life. You are a life force moving along with other life forces. As you recognize this, you open up and draw near to these others, becoming more and more one with them, working together for My purposes.*

The devas themselves have no particular form. But in attempting to establish communication and cooperation with humans, members of the devic realms have made themselves visible in a form intelligible to humans. These forms reflect their functions. For instance, a dwarf is usually depicted with a pickaxe, denoting our human interpretation of his work with the mineral world. Angels, on the other hand, are portrayed with wings, and often as bearing something, such as a message of healing or mercy. As the devas have said, *We work in the formless worlds and are not bound or rigid in form as you are. We travel from realm to realm and are given wings to denote this movement. As we travel, our form changes, taking on the qualities of different realms. Therefore, you cannot pin us down to any one form. We deal directly with energy and that energy shapes us, is part of us,* ***is*** *us, until we breathe it out to where it is needed. We are limitless, free, and insubstantial.*

I have never seen any of these beings in a definite form, although sometimes I get an impression of a pattern, a shape or a color. Once

when I had the image of the Red Cabbage Deva standing in front of many vague forms, I was told, *These forms are myself and those like me as we have been and as we shall be. Although we live in the moment and are always moving, yet is our past and present with us. We are close to the inner realms where all is living. I give you this picture so that you will not see me, or any of us, as merely one of a list of static forms but will connect us up more with life. Humans are so inclined to limit and depend upon their five senses to perceive the world that they forget that we are living, changing forces* <u>*now*</u>*, outside your sense of time.*

As we became more aware of the fact that everything around us is part of the same energy in different forms, we were opened up to an entirely new way of working in the garden. The devas said, *We realize it is easy for man to think of a plant as a thing, perhaps as living, but nevertheless a thing, for he cuts himself off from the vision that sees beyond the physical, just as he cuts himself off from his own inner being which is so vast.* Taking into account the inner being of plants, we began to realize that the garden must be known from within as well as from without, that it must grow spiritually as well as physically.

To a deva, the garden is not an assembly of various forms and colors but rather moving lines of energy. In describing our garden they said they could see the forces from below gradually being drawn up and blending with those coming down from them in great, swift waves. Within this field of energy, each plant was an individual whirlpool of activity. *We do not see things as you do, in their solid, outer materializations, but rather in their inner life-giving state. We deal with what is behind what you see or sense, but these are interconnected, like different octaves of the same melody. What we see is different forms of light.* Years later, when I read about Kirlian photography, which records the luminescence given off by matter, I felt this related to the subtler forces of which the devas speak.

The devas stressed the importance of our learning to see the true reality, as they do, so that we might with the power of our directed thought not only affirm the perfection of each plant but actually lift it to a higher level. *By thinking in terms of light, you add light to that already existing. Hence, you speed up growth and enhance beauty, you see truth and link up with God's perfection.* The intention of the devas in introducing us to their way of seeing was not to detract from the beauty of the world as seen by human eyes, but to enhance it by expanding our awareness into a broader and truer perception.

In time, we learned that thinking in this way was indeed a practical way of working in the garden. But at first, being wise teachers, the devas responded to what was most obviously vital to us at the moment—the actual physical needs of the garden, only gradually introducing us to this new

perception. They gave us specific advice, for instance, on how far apart plants should be or where to place them. *We think that the land on the top there would be a good site for us, as long as it is not too windy,* the Globe Artichoke Deva advised. The Cabbage Deva suggested, *It would be better to thin out the plants now. Also taking off those lower leaves will be alright.* In springtime, the Blackcurrant Deva told us, *No, don't cut the plants back now. The root would not be strengthened if you did; it needs the leaves to make the process of life go through the plant.*

We used to gather sheep dung from a nearby field to make a liquid fertilizer. *Liquid manure is a great medium for certain ranges of forces, because liquid attracts and gathers in certain subtle forces which cannot enter into a more solid medium,* a deva informed us, and advised, *The strength is about right, although for certain plants it could be a little stronger.* I used to do regular rounds with the liquid manure, asking each vegetable deva whether or not the plants would like a dose that day. Sometimes the response was just a direct *Yes* or *No*, while at other times it was combined with a bit of general information. Asking the Tomato Deva about nutrients, I got, *You can give the plant liquid manure now. We will not let all the goodness of it be used for developing leaves. When there is cooperation between us like this, we can give instructions to the plant that it is the fruit which is to be developed.* The Carrot Deva told us, *The carrots are coming along nicely and could be missed when you put on another dose of liquid manure. You wonder why they are alright when the parsnips next to them are hungry. The carrots, through their special carrot quality, are able to convert energy from the radiations which parsnips do not tune into.*

The soil, of course, was one of the areas of our garden that received a great deal of attention. In transforming sand into soil, we were re-enacting the natural process of creation on our planet by drawing together the ingredients necessary to sustain life. The day following my first contact with the Pea Deva, I was told in guidance that we could ask questions about the soil from a certain being overlighting our geographical area. We were told that the magnetism of this angel and the magnetism of the land around us were linked and interacted. For want of a better name, we called this being the Landscape Angel. I got an initial impression of it with "hands" outstretched, passing energy into the ground. *You can see me juggling the life forces into the garden and never ceasing the movement. We work in what you call mantras, in movements, which produce sound and make a pattern, working up to a certain pitch. By these moves, I am now putting a certain quality of life force into the garden. There are many irregularities in the composition of the soil and by adding these explosions of forces, they are being minimized.* For about two years, we were given almost daily guidance from the Landscape Angel on how to build compost and enrich the soil. For instance, we were told, *You have a real difficulty with that soil which does need more air but which would blow away if you loosened it. If possible, hoe it before a rain and loosen it before spreading compost on it.*

The devas said, viewing it from the angle of energy, that the greatest physical contribution to the garden was the compost heap. We were given specific advice as to what ingredients to use, when to mix each individual heap, and when and where to spread the ripened mixture. For instance, the Landscape Angel told us, *It would be good to turn the remainder of that first compost heap, but the other one is not quite ready for turning—a week or so, and then start building the others. We can tell by the degree of radiance that the one heap needs attention—it has dulled down. The others are still building up to the point where they should be moved.*

Spreading compost throughout the garden brought the whole area into greater unity. *It is a binding, uniting process, like the circulation of the blood in the body.* Our ignorance in these areas is obvious to any gardener, but because of it we were able to accept the advice we received from the devas, see the successful results, and then open ourselves to what they had to teach us further about life.

However, working in cooperation with humans was pioneering for the devas as well, and so they could not always foresee what would happen in the garden. Our first season, the broad beans started out in an energetic flowering, but then the blossoms began falling off. When I asked the deva why this was happening, I received, *To tell the truth, we threw ourselves fully into our cooperation with you and did not allow for the quality of the soil. The shot in the arm given us through your collaboration shot us ahead too fast! So we are balancing up this way. We have no regrets; it was well worth trying.* They were always willing to experiment. I think this was sometimes done so that we would learn the true effects of certain actions and gardening practices.

In our garden, they did not feel limited, and they could see the creative power of humans, so they wanted to show what could be done with their cooperation. A wonderful example of this was our work with the Watercress Deva. Various gardening books were sharply divided on how to grow watercress. While one said it could not be done without running water, another said it could if grown in the shade, and yet a third advised growing it in the sun. Unsure of what to do, Peter asked me to contact the deva, who suggested that we experiment by growing half in the shade and half in the sun. This proved wise advice because, with daily watering, the plants in the sun grew quickly, providing us with watercress throughout the summer and then went to seed just as the plants in the shade were ready for picking in late summer and autumn.

It delighted the devas when Peter acted on their suggestions. While at the beginning of our contact they had seemed rather remote, our cooperation changed that, and they became friendly and even anxious to help. In fact, we were told that they were practically queueing up to experience this new contact with human life. They said that the few contacts made with Western man in the past had not usually been happy ones, except for those made by gardeners who truly loved plants. Contacts had also been made to bring about new plant forms, yet the horticultural experts who were responsible for these innovations had not always worked with the nature forces as equal partners but sometimes imposed their will on nature, making it respond to their designs. So although the devas welcomed our questions as a means to bring about understanding and true cooperation between us, what interested them most was the process by which a human—deaf, dumb and blind in their regions—was reaching out to know them and talk to them.

Both in the guidance Eileen received and in messages from the devas, we were told to grow as many varieties in our garden as possible. Besides producing a better balance in the soil, a large variety of plants focused the forces of more devas. That in turn attracted the great overlighting devas who could use the garden to serve a certain purpose on the planet. Peter was ordering vegetables and herbs we had not seen or heard of until the nursery catalogues brought them to our notice—plants with strange names like celeriac, salsify and scorzonera, kohlrabi and cardoon, soapwort and sweet cicely. The herbs we ordered were sent to us by rail, beautifully packed in moss and cellophane and we carefully planted them out in our garden. As they grew, we discovered that sweet cicely was one of the commonest roadside "weeds" in the area!

As Peter brought each new plant into the garden, I welcomed the deva of its species. I found each had a unique feeling and quality. The Radish Deva, who has always been especially active in the

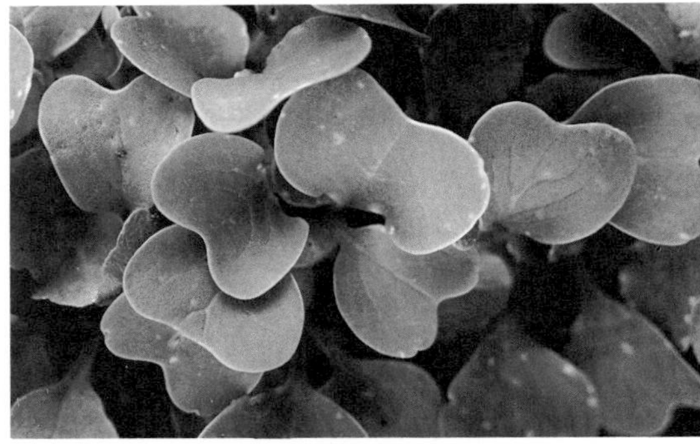

garden at Findhorn, responded to my welcome with, *We swoop in again, delighted to spread ourselves. We are in a great hurry it seems to you. Our forces give the impression of eager beavers. We are that, but with hearts too!* The Angelica Deva

on the other hand was a bit more hesitant: *We come in quietly, intent on our small world. To be asked to speak is unusual, to say the least, but you feel our influence and we hope that the particular quality with which you respond to us will be greatly strengthened here. Thus is our mission on Earth fulfilled.*

Most often the devas exhibited a quality of exuberance and vitality, as did the Marrow Deva: *We are delighted to be given so much space and should like to be able to throw great hefty marrows straight into your laps! But if we did that, we should not daily be making use of the available forces given us for growth through nature and man. The growing process is a great blessing in itself. It is creation, and perhaps it is difficult at times, but everything is used for that purpose and the greater good. We are glad to be a part of it, glad to grow for you.* When we decided to grow dandelions as a vegetable, the deva responded, *I am greatly honored to come into the garden by the front door! It does make a difference in the bond between us and man when we come at his desire*

instead of in spite of him, for with his aid the struggle is not so great and the plant can expand and do its best. Let us show what we can do in cooperation. Nevertheless, I hope to be greeting you from odd corners. Cooperation indeed made a vast difference, because the dandelions we welcomed in grew to a relatively great size.

I find that I have to know something of a new plant before being able to contact the deva. Often I would read about the characteristics of a plant—or sometimes taste a bit of it. This was not always an enjoyable encounter! Sampling a wormwood leaf, I was quite taken aback by the strength of its flavor, and I can't say I would recommend the

experience. The deva responded, *You are amazed that such a strong taste can be contained in such a little bit of leaf. Power is our nature—a little root can crack rocks. Power can be used for many purposes. You humans also have power. Yet power is a word which many people shy away from because in human hands it can be used for evil. Power is said to corrupt. We view it in another light entirely. We consider it the greatest gift of God because with it we can do more for God than without it. It is our joy to perfect that power in*

service. Because the herb devas concentrate all their energy in expressing one particular essence, the flavors of these plants are very distinct.

I found the herb devas especially amenable to contact with humans. *Plants such as us, the herbs, have long associations with humans and are thus ready to be leaders in the cooperation between our two worlds. We are part of human consciousness. You have discovered much about us and we can easily dance into your awareness. But remember, this is a new contact on a new level and not one from which you can compile dictionaries of long words about our abilities. I do not mean that we will not give you information about our use, but the contact comes when you rise to a level of joy and purity. You must respect us and love us as part of God's life before we can trust you with more secrets about ourselves. Plants are not here just for man's use, but when you learn that man's chief end is to glorify God and enjoy him forever, then we can be part of that enjoyment and glorification, each in our own way, in your consciousness.*

Each herb, we were told, embodied a particular quality or radiance. As we eat them that quality is enhanced in ourselves. Thus, the wider the range of herbs we eat, the more help they can give us. Gradually we became familiar with all those growing in our garden, mostly by eating them in various combinations in our daily salads.

When flowers were introduced into the garden, I found it easiest to contact each deva if the plant was in bloom, for at that time its essence was in fullest manifestation. With certain flowers I felt a natural closeness. The Mesembryanthemum Deva, in particular, felt just like a sister to me. Since the petals of this flower unfold only in the sun, this may be the link, because I, too, have a great love for the sun. With others, if I had difficulty feeling any unique characteristics, I sometimes even picked a bloom and kept it in my room for a while until I made its acquaintance. Straining for the contact only created a barrier. *What will come to you will come as on the wings of song, effortlessly,* the devas told me.

By springtime of our second year at Findhorn, the Landscape Angel told us that our garden was becoming more united and whole, and that as this took place, an angelic being, a sort of guardian angel for our area, was forming. I believe that any unit, whether it be a farm or a community, a couple or a nation, has an overlighting presence that in some way embodies the various levels of energy used within that unit. The Angel of Findhorn is a composite being, "born" from the substance of our thoughts and ideals, the radiations of the land, and the energies of the higher selves of not only the humans working on the land but of all the animals and plants there as well.

Each step of its development was described to us by the Landscape Angel. *The being forming here is a new type of deva. This is becoming increasingly apparent. It is gathering life from all of you in a unity with humankind hitherto unknown. You are in a sense part of its body. It will act as a bridge between you and others of my kingdom, and will help you in your work.*

At this point it is still nebulous. Although to you it may be slow in growing, it is phenomenally fast compared with others. You cannot feel this new creature yet; nor can we, but we sense it being brought about. Its eyes are still closed, so to speak, its reposeful hands still being defined. Its length is very great. Definite warmth directed to it will speed up the process and quicken its life.

A month later, when our garden had been further extended, the Landscape Angel said that the eyes of the new deva were open and that the head had some movement. However, it could not be fully formed until one complete round of plant growth—a year—had passed; otherwise it would not incorporate all the energies necessary for the garden.

When at last it was fully formed, the Findhorn Angel presented itself to us: *I take my stand with my brothers, tall and one in essence. Immensely vigorous and vital am I with a role that reaches to the four corners of the Earth and beyond. We all rejoice amongst ourselves in these realms that, with the help of all of you, has been born and grown to fulfillment one such as I, a prototype of cooperative activity. I have been planned from near the Godhead and given sustenance by both the deva and human worlds. Do not form a clear concept of me and keep me in limitation.*

Now I go from your consciousness, but I am in you and you are in me, different yet one. I am the spirit of a place, yet how much more. You are limited human beings, but you are gods in the making. We are one because we have all been given life.

Our cooperation with nature was not only affecting our human world, but the devic realms were also changing through it. The devas exist in the world of the One, without question carrying out the will of God. Because they allow the power to come through them unrestricted, they are, in a sense, more powerful than man. On the other hand,

man, living in the world of opposites has freedom of choice and thus the power to create. Yet we are evolving towards each other, the devas into understanding how separation can enhance awareness and appreciation, and humans into participating once again in the consciousness of the unity of all life.

Expressing the new awareness brought about in their realms by contact with us, the devas said: *We have told you that we are one in essence, that we melt into one another at any time. Whereas that quality has not changed, to it has been added an ability to look at one another, as it were. This brings about a greater sharing, for it is easy to be one if you are not separate! Now our praises can ring higher and deeper, our wonder can mount, in this wider awareness of the forces of life.* For us humans, broader awareness comes by recognizing our oneness with all aspects of life. *You consider us beings of light and joy, which we are, but you seldom consider humans as beings of light, which you are. As you encompass all worlds, including ours, when you drop your burdens and become a creature of light, you are one with us.*

The primary impact on me of the deva world has been this necessity to rise to a higher state within myself in order to contact them. If I am depressed, angry, resentful or caught in some negative emotional state, I cannot enter the light and joyous atmosphere of their realms. *You cannot bring weights into our world, you cannot come to us unless you are free, child-like and light. If you choose, you can live your everyday life in the very same attitude which you bring to us. You know you have to drop your burdens to contact us and therefore you know you can do it. We say, why not do it all the time? It seems strange to keep*

on the old way when freedom is yours at any time you choose. You love the feel of our life; why not live in it more often?

As I attune to the devas, I partake of their qualities. It is as if they sound a tuning fork that awakens a response within me—their joy and mine become one, and I find I am a joyous being. So every contact with the devas becomes an expansion of my own highest spirit.

I have been mainly speaking of the devas as spirits of nature. But they also embody qualities of the human spirit, such as perseverance, tolerance and courage. *One of our biggest roles in helping humans is to hold in absolute purity and perfection some quality, so that you may come and be steeped in it and carry its essence within to help you in life's ways.* The deva world has always been part of man's highest endeavors, his moments of inspiration and adoration, of wonder and enchantment. What the devas have said to me, wise men have expressed in many ways throughout the ages. This wisdom is the spirit within us calling to us through every part of life, within and without, whether in the song of an angel or the voice of a babbling brook.

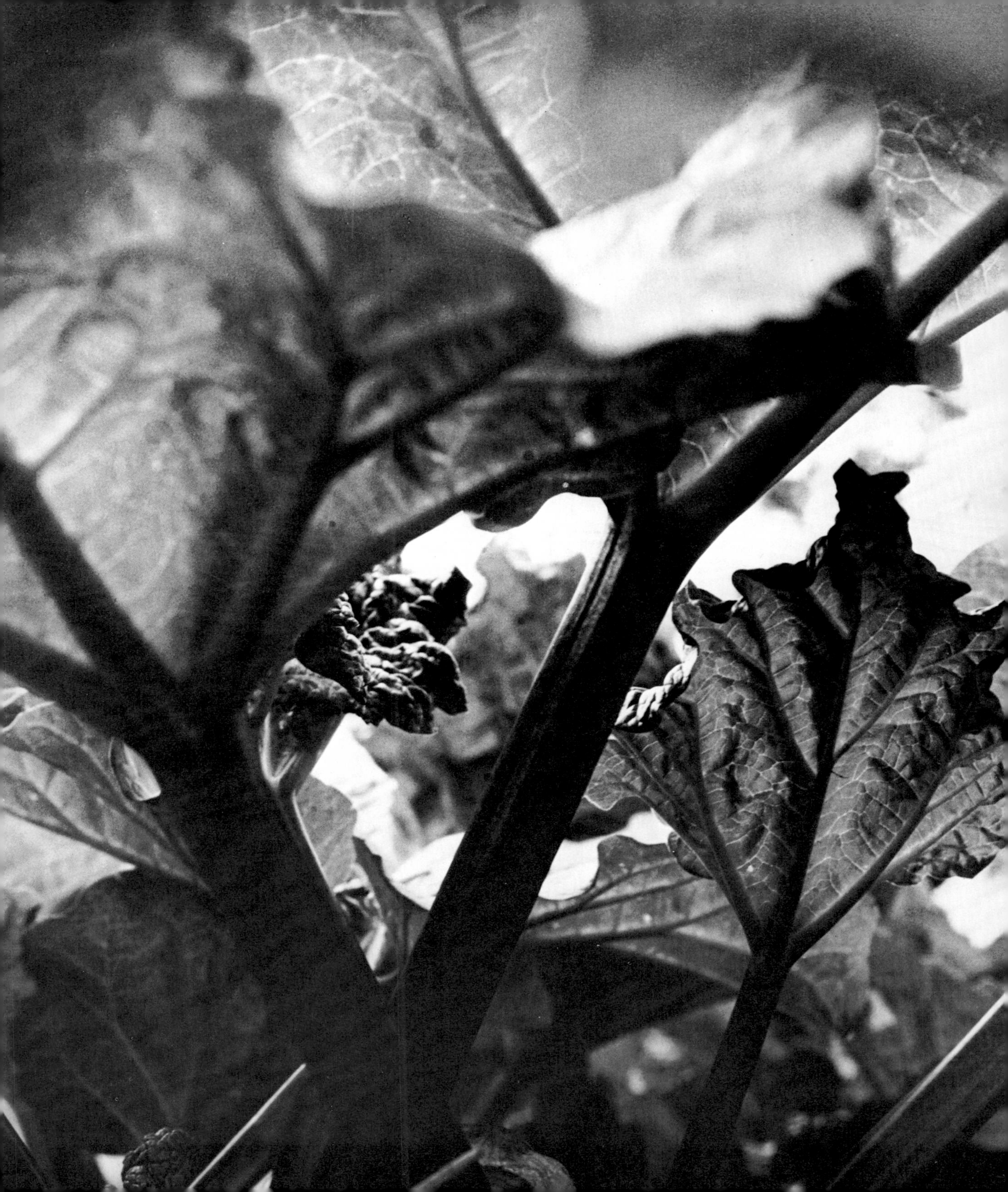

While the kingdom of the devas exists as a life unto itself, they are also part of us. In fact, to the consciousness that is expanded enough, all things are within. *How can oneness be if you reach outside yourself for it? If God—who is all—is within, can you exclude us? Be sensible.* As our consciousness grows, we cannot help but be aware of the devas, for contacting them is basically the same as being in contact with our true selves.

All of us have experienced the devas in one way or another. In fact, they say that any contact with the plant world puts us in touch with their realms. When I first contacted the Rhubarb Deva, I was told: *We have met before. Whenever anyone contributes attention or feeling to a plant, a bit of that person's being mingles with a bit of our being, and the one world is fostered. You humans are therefore all very linked to us, but until you give recognition to these links, they are as nothing and remain undeveloped. The plants contribute to human food and give of themselves in this way. This also builds links, tangible ones. Although of the past, these links can be brought into the present by recalling them. This is one great use for memory, to recall the oneness of life.* To firmly establish these links, it is important to appreciate and enjoy the food we eat. *Our essence goes into your being much more readily when our flavor is enjoyed,* the Winter Savory Deva said. *That way you are open to our influence and let it spread through you.*

To contact the deva world, an interchange in word or thought is not necessary. Just as everyone responds to a person or a thing according to his or her own particular make-up and perhaps mood at the time, there are infinite levels of communication with the devas. Whenever we are in a state of joy, love, lightness, freedom, we are with the devas. When we are lifted out of ourselves, looking into the beauty of a flower or a sunset or the amazing shape of a shell, this is an experience of the deva world. *Consciousness of beauty brings you into oneness with any part of the universe,* they have said. My great love for being outdoors, in touch with the sun, the wind and rain was contact with the devic realms. But only when I had a conscious request from within to contact these beings, did I become aware of their existence.

Recognizing their world is most important. This had a tremendous effect on our garden. The devas told us, *Forces work through us into the soil, and extra strength is given them by your consciousness of them. Everything belongs to one world, but if each thing or life lives to itself, it cuts itself off from the one great teeming force field. If each opens out to the all, then currents flow through unhindered. So realize that your recognition of us opens up strength to us and to you, because it lets the forces flow naturally.*

Considerations we had hitherto thought impractical in the garden, the devas insisted were eminently practical. Our attitudes, thoughts and feelings had a great effect on the plants, they said. Knowing this had a great effect on us, as well, since we had to learn to be careful about how we felt, how we spoke and what we did around the garden. If we were not in a good state, it was best to go elsewhere. We began to realize the truth of what the devas were telling us: *Every creature, human or otherwise, reacts to and acts upon its environment (quite unwittingly sometimes) for all is one.*

The devas told us that since their purpose was to increase life, they couldn't tell us how to destroy the insects that were eating our plants. However, they said that by visualizing the plants as strong and healthy we could add to their life force and thus help them to withstand the attack. The power of such thought was clearly revealed to me one year when our gooseberry bushes were beset by a plague of caterpillars. Left alone, the insects would have completely stripped off all the young leaves. So I took it upon myself to help out by plucking the little creatures off each bush. This wasn't easy, considering my secret horror of caterpillars. Never before in my life had I even touched one. I would steel myself and spend hours on end collecting caterpillars into a jar, and then deposit them on top of the compost heap where the birds would eat them. It was the best solution I could think of.

One day in the middle of this task, I realized that I was so engrossed in the caterpillars that I had forgotten all about the gooseberry bushes themselves. During the rest of that round, I made a point of beaming out thoughts of love and health to the bushes. Next time I went on my rounds, I noticed that those bushes which had received love actually had far fewer caterpillars on them than those which I had not given specific attention to. It was an illuminating experience.

A further and more trying test of my faith in the power of thought came during our first year at Findhorn. Because of all the compost we were spreading around the garden, we were beginning to have great luscious earthworms—just what moles like. All around us was sand and gravel, so into our garden the moles came, rooting around in our patio and other areas, leaving the roots of the poor plants hanging in the air, unable to get water or sustenance. Peter came to me and said, "Moles—do something about them." Not knowing quite what to do, I decided I might try to use my inner contact.

Concentrating on the essence of a mole, I received the impression of a rather scary Great King Mole with a crown on his head sitting in an underground cavern. Feeling rather diffident, I began, "Well, we have a garden and you moles are upsetting it. Can't you do something about it?" I just presented the situation to him fairly, suggesting that they go to a neighboring area of land not being used for gardening. There was nothing more I could do. I gave him my promise that I would not harm him or any of the moles. He just sort of grunted and said, "Hmmmm," and I was left unsure whether this had helped at all. But for several weeks there was no sign of moles in the garden. Each time they reappeared, I repeated my plea to the Mole King. By the end of that season, they had all left the garden and didn't return.

However, several years later, when Findhorn was given the neighboring area of land, there they all were, just where we had asked them to go. By then I was no longer working in the garden, but I told the group of gardeners about my experience. Together, using the same technique, they contacted the moles and got an even swifter response than I had received by myself—and the garden remained mole free. This showed me that everyone can use that inner attunement to all aspects of life to work in cooperation with nature, rather than relying on destructive solutions.

Despite years of relating to the garden, I never developed into what I would call a real gardener.

When you are near a plant and in its aura, as when you are under a tree, for instance, you are fed its radiations. When you eat of the plant you are fed its radiations on another level of your being. One method can be as important as the other. This is another reason for spending time in the garden.

Therefore, I cannot give a gardener's answers to gardening concerns; I can only give devic answers. Hopefully, as our consciousness expands into greater awareness, these will be the same.

In the Findhorn garden, we saw what the cooperation of humans and devas could bring about, each realm contributing a unique and vital energy. But the implications of such cooperation extend far beyond simply growing successful gardens. At a time when it appears that material solutions to ecological crises are not sufficient, perhaps the devas are offering us a real alternative on how to restore the upset balance of nature on our planet. *We know that if humanity could get the feel of our realms, life on Earth would be completely changed.* As wielders of energy, they are offering their help in making our world as light and joyful as theirs. But as they have told us again and again, we must play our part, using the power of our free will to direct the energy creatively, both within ourselves and in the world around us. Each one of us can consciously choose to function beyond our current limitations and use the energy he or she has for a larger purpose. And we can find joy and satisfaction in the growing awareness that each one's contribution is of importance, no matter how small it may seem.

The key to this transformation lies in recognizing that oneness of all life of which the devas continually remind us. *When you come to us we would not keep you, so to speak, but pass you on in consciousness to the One of whom we are ever conscious, who is our life and the light of the world.* This is the basic teaching of the devas, guiding each of us to our inner core, to the divinity within, from which we go out in harmony with all of life.

If we can thus transform our way of looking at life, our actions within our environment will be transformed. *Man drastically changes the face of the Earth as it suits him, without a thought that he is dealing with God's life, in various forms. To him it is just shifting matter around. But if he thought of everything in terms of light, all shining with the substance of God, he would not so carelessly alter the Earth.* As we begin to recognize God in every aspect of the world around us, that part of the world is redeemed, until ultimately the whole planet is redeemed.

We humans are supremely gifted. We can encompass the entire range of life on our planet, and it is our destiny to do so. We begin by becoming more and more of what we are, more of what the devas are. *We have often expressed to you our great joy as you turn to our kingdom, and we have come flocking with our power and bestowed much on your garden. We would pour down on you all, activating what you already have within, some characteristics of the angelic world: our abounding joy, our lightness, our vitality, our freedom, our flexibility. We could go on and on, for there is no end to God's gifts to his creation. In all this we are one, without separation. Let us extend that oneness to all levels, and let us do it here and now.*

THE MESSAGES. Every plant does have a unique ensouling presence. These messages, however, have not been communicated by individual plants but rather by the overlighting intelligence and spirit—the deva—for each plant species. While the devas themselves are beyond form, yet are they responsible for the most precise and minute forms we behold in the plant kingdom, the wonderful exactness of each seed and leaf and blossom. This they do in joy and lightness, as the great servers of life.

The process by which I contact the devas is one of feeling into the essence of a plant and harmonizing my own self with it. The communication doesn't come to me as words, but as thoughts of inspiration, which I then express in words according to my own state of consciousness at the time. If I were to receive the same communication now, I probably would not word it in the same way, for my consciousness, as is only natural, has grown into a deeper understanding and awareness.

Because each garden is unique, the devas did not give general rules of action. As they told me, *Humans know most of these from the traditions of gardening. It is in the field of conscious-sharing that something new is to be learned.* Moreover, they wanted us to find out for ourselves what it is that we as humans are capable of doing. We have all knowledge within ourselves, they have said, and they would point us toward that.

To me, one of the most significant aspects of contact with the devas is simply that it helps to enlarge our viewpoint. If we treat everything as alive, intelligent and part of the One Life, our own life is greatly enriched. When we realize that we are in a sea of life with which we can communicate, there is bound to be cooperation between mankind and nature.

As we grow to understand that the key to contacting the devic realms is to seek within, to be what we truly are, we will discover that the devas are a part of our very selves.

COMMUNICATION

Love-lies-bleeding Deva
24 October 1968
You translate what I pass on to you with your own understanding. That is the way all consciousness grows, like a plant reaching up for support, finding and grasping it, growing and then reaching again. Someone else might put the ideas quite differently. Each is free to understand in his own terms.

Clematis Deva
6 June 1970
It does not matter through which part of creation you contact our kingdom, whether by way of a flower in full display as I am now, attracting you with a solid wall of soft color and scent, or by way of a little clover leaf, a wisp of wind, a drop of rain, or the sun itself. All have the breath of God in them. The air you breathe—is it not full of God, is it not your life force? All of creation shares in it, contributes something to it.

You cannot separate life into parts; all is of the Divine. When you come to any of us who are causal factors of manifestation, you are bound to come closer to God and closer to the oneness of life. It is perhaps easier to see good in the unblemished beauty of a flower because you humans separate things into good and evil, but when you delve deeply into anything you will find God is there.

The Devas
1 May 1972
Just tune into nature until you feel the love flow. That is your arrow into the deva world. It does not matter if there is a message or not, it is the state which counts. Always it is your state that the nature world responds to, not what you say, not what you do, but what you are.

Landscape Angel
27 April 1967
Your love for our kingdom joins us to humans. You see, there are no individual egos with us; when you love one beech tree, for example, you love all beech trees, you are connected with the whole genus of beech. Even though it may be one particular specimen that brings out the love in you, that specimen is incapable of taking your regard to itself, and thus you are automatically linked up with the spirit of that species. If the human kingdom could learn this quality, it would mean the end of war and rivalry, competition and strife.

You are in the world of action where we are not physically embodied, and that is your great opportunity and privilege. You are the outer extension of ourselves as we are the inner extensions of you. Let the oneness grow in your awareness.

The Devas
22 May 1964
Soar up with us and feel the bewitching strength of life's radiations as we know them. These are the radiations which we pour through the plants and which the plants bring to you. As you concentrate in peace and stretch your being up to these radiations, as you become sensitive to them on our level, you become more sensitive to them in the plants. Their essence is easier for you to touch on the inner planes with us leading you to them, but let our contact lead you to the outer world and let the outer lead you to the inner until all is one.

The Devas
22 June 1971
Love is a firm reality which forms a bridge over which all can walk. Gooey sentiment is not love and does not exist with us. When we step towards you, we do it energetically; you can do the same. Though you cannot see, hear, touch, smell or taste us, we are a tremendous force. We stand here in love, a whole dynamic world ready for an intelligent relationship with the humanity that will wield all God-given forces for the whole.

Pear Deva
13 March 1965
To you I am a being of great beauty because you contact the reality of me: a being which is God, free, happy and expressing his perfect life. Yet that rather spindly tree growing in the garden is my expression. Of course you know that in blossom time the inner beauty is more apparent, and also the fruit is a form which is clearly unique to me. Nevertheless, you think this tree is but a limited expression of me.

Come nearer and feel a oneness with the tree. Slip into its limbs and feel the same unity that the tree spirit feels with it. Feel how the spirit loves the tree, how it is the tree. We are one.

You were one with us in that moment. We believe that as you reach into our life like that, as we achieve greater unity, Heaven will be brought down to Earth.

THE GARDENERS

Landscape Angel
17 October 1969
We would have you love the garden and all in it, putting your care and attention to it. But above all we would have you feel it all part of the One. It is not enough to grow plants merely for beauty, appearance or use. Grow them also because all are expressions of the whole.

You, too, are parts of the whole—part of that clod of earth, part of that tiny flower, part of the sunshine and the rain, the light in another's eye, the warmth of another's smile. And you are part of us, the angelic hosts who overlight and give life to the planet, who care for you all, though you know it not.

Landscape Angel
31 May 1963
The personal qualities of a gardener can be used by the nature forces to add to plant growth. For example, Peter's radiations are forceful and purposeful and are used a great deal. Every gardener contributes to his garden in this way, but those consciously aligned to the Great Provider can be used much more.

Certain people stimulate plant growth, others have a depressing effect and even draw upon the plant forces. Happiness has an especially good effect on plants, as do children at play.

Your radiations and the radiations of the plants are more

interwoven than you realize, for although the nature spirits shy away from humans, they cannot help but be affected by human vibrations for they are open creatures without the many skins humans have.

Landscape Angel
20 June 1963
We see life in terms of the inner force while you see only the outer form and cannot see the continual process taking place. We should like you to try to think in our terms, because it will make things easier for both of us—you will be closer to reality and will also be able to understand us better.

These inner forces are as intricate as the outer form, having shape, color, texture, etc., but of a finer and richer substance. When you look at plants, know that what you see has an inner counterpart simply pulsating with the life you see and much more. As your mind becomes more familiar with this concept and you think of the plants as glowing and moving with life, you will in fact add to that life. By thought, you add to their force and at the same time you draw upon the Source of all life, generating more and more power and more and more life. That is what we all want.

Landscape Angel
30 July 1964
Rain, having passed through many radiations as part of a natural process, is far better for plants than watering. But when man does find it necessary to water, he can give out radiations which are as helpful to the plants as the natural ones that come with the rain. When man acts as part of the one life, he is that and is a transformer for many ranges of vibrations. The plants are grateful for the water and especially for the love that can come with it.

Spinach Deva
16 June 1963
As your thoughts create order and unity, as they become more aligned with the whole, so will the forces in the garden become more aligned as well, and what does not fit in will drop out. As you positively hold perfection for each plant in your mind so will it be brought into form.

We are able to work most effectively when we have your creative thought with us, protecting and feeding each plant. It is your garden, you are the creators of it, and we only help as each seed or plant needs it. The overall result depends on your inner strength as put forth in the garden.

The gardens of the future will far surpass anything known at present, not because science and intelligence aid or promote them but because love does. The sensitivity and sharing of love, the oneness it brings, makes the plant more fully what it is, more fully its God-essence.

COOPERATION

The Devas
26 January 1969
If mankind's cooperation with the deva world is to grow, you should realize more of what we do. The more God's creatures know of one another the greater the unity and peace.

Landscape Angel
12 July 1963
There are many units in my care, places where the owners have a great love for their gardens and where "guardians" from the devic realms exist. But unless man is conscious of the divine in him and acts from it, he is open to error and his work falls short of perfection. Until man is conscious of our existence and recognizes the part we play in the formation of the worlds on which he depends, there is no true cooperation. Even if he has no link with us through direct contact, the fact of affirming our existence forms a link and is part of the truth on which to build. In your recognition of and cooperation with us, we realize anew the increased play of forces this engenders.

Landscape Angel
28 July 1964
In the tremendous growth in the garden, you have evidence in form of how power when recognized is made manifest. We of the deva world have been contacted, recognized by you, and thus given "hands and feet" which we would otherwise not have. As power within you is not awakened until it is recognized and called forth, so must you call forth our powers.

Landscape Angel
31 October 1969
We come when there is a call from any part of life. But the initiative must come from your side. We do not force ourselves on you. We rejoice at man's cooperation but the rejoicing is because he is reaching out to us. We have always been part of life on Earth and of man's endeavors, but man has been generally unaware of our part. Now his consciousness is broadening to truth and of course we rejoice.

Lettuce Deva
25 June 1963
We can cooperate in many ways. For example, we can control the life force in individual plants, speed it up or slow it down. Our work is not merely setting the life force in action, like winding up a clock, and then leaving the plants to finish the course as best they can, but rather we carefully control each step. We have been given certain powers, and within our limits we wield them. In your experiment let us aid you all we can.

THE PATTERN

Tomato Deva
7 August 1963
Each plant has a pattern which it follows. While circumstances, weather conditions, food, availability, etc. may alter that pattern, we bring about its manifestation according to its design and the materials available. It is not our work to initiate a change of pattern or evolve new ones. Eagerly we follow our plan of perfection, but we cannot reach down and control the material plane. That is the work of man. We simply use conditions to bring about evolution. But man is capable of changing these conditions.

Angel of Sound

3 July 1963

Each plant sounds a note which attracts its builders to it and calls substance to itself through the nature spirits. We devas know the individual notes for all in our charge, and we sound them, like tuning forks, to be picked up by each plant. When a seed is ready to germinate, moisture and warmth do not of themselves set its note vibrating—we do that. We set the seed on its way and hold out its note before it to follow. That note changes with growth and stages, as does man whose voice changes as he advances into maturity.

Apple Deva

26 May 1970

You feel drawn to us by the clustered blossom and the promise of fruit to come. That from a fragile, scarcely colored and shortlived bloom, a sturdy rosy apple appears is but one of God's miracles enacted many times over for all to observe. If you could see more of how this is brought about by the chain of life, wonder would lift you high.

As from the seed a tree grows, so from the seed idea a pattern issues forth from the Center, passed on by silent ranks of angels—silent and still because that idea is still too unformed and unfixed to endure any but the most exacting care. Growing in strength and size, the pattern becomes brighter until eventually it scintillates and sounds, still in the care of the outermost great angel. Its forcefield is steady and brilliant.

Then the pattern is passed on to the elements, the makers of form. They give of themselves to clothe that pattern. Remember, this is a process; the pattern is apparent everywhere in the ethers, held by the angels and made manifest beyond time. Then at the appropriate opportunity, through the ministrations of the nature spirits, it appears in time and place, in the beauty of the

The nature kingdoms need their champions to help redress the balance that has been upset by man. However, true balance is not a position of rigidity but one of great ease, a flowing with every moment, giving, taking and adjusting, constantly seeking oneness.

blossom and the succulence of the fruit.

This is the Word made flesh, this is all creation, held in balance by great layers of life of which your conscious mind is unaware. A miracle? You need a greater word, you need to go beyond words.

The fruits of the earth are produced through the unsung and dedicated service of these many forms of life. We hope that the gardeners at your end of the line are as happy in their work! You, man, have the fruits, although you do only a small part of the work. May your praise be greater than ours which never ceases.

Love-lies bleeding Deva
24 October 1968
Life itself is growth, and we must be free to keep up with it, to hold or change our pattern as the need may be. We are not an assembly line endlessly churning out identical objects, for life is ceaselessly growing, moving on, learning, rising and becoming more and more conscious.

SOIL

Landscape Angel
27 April 1967
Soil is the very substance of this planet, refined through aeons of time, the seedbed of life at the disposal of all and every life. You say "cleanliness is next to godliness," and you wash earth off your hands, while at the same time you pollute that earth with that which annuls life. It is right that you should be clean of surplus matter, but it is also right that we should have clean matter to fulfill our function.

Landscape Angel
14 December 1968
It makes an enormous difference to the soil when you work it with love, when you handle it with love, think of it and the life in it with love. Then you are channeling into the soil higher energy and imbuing it with God-power. You see, the matter in it, the life in it, does not have great consciousness of God, but this is where man can transform the earth. He can fairly pepper it with higher vibrations and thereby entirely raise its level. He can work with us in this aspect and raise all life, raise the whole tone of life on this planet.

Landscape Angel
6 October 1963
It is good to put compost into the soil as often as possible, however small the amounts, because you are adding life force from the compost and yourself. We are working on your soil all the time, and as you add more ingredients, we have more scope. We are even more delighted than you to see the soil becoming rich, bright and united.

I am using words not generally applied to the soil, but more and more, as your thinking grows, we can use these truer terms. Of course, the terms for physical and spiritual beauty overlap.

Millions of years nature took to make the soil rich, but in a very short space you will do the same.

Landscape Angel
15 August 1969
I have often told you to think of plants in terms of life, shining life, because this is what they are. Likewise the soil. To us it is a mass of life, each tiny cell or group of cells with a function in the overall plan of life.

The life force in the soil comes through the soil population. It is as though first there was darkness, or inert matter, and then there was light. The light transformed the darkness without which the light could not exist, because darkness, matter, is its mother, its very substance. The transforming of matter or minerals into a form capable of a higher vibrational level, what you call evolution, begins at the lowest level and continues up to the highest.

The soil population plays a vital part in this. The natural way a plant pattern comes into form is by using soil, water, heat and air. All these are drawn up into form by the invisible workers in the elements. These you call soil population on one level, fairies on another level. The necessary elements in soil are materialized through fungi; that is why in myths fairies and toadstools are connected.

When humans wish to create with controlled thought, according to how strongly they hold the pattern in their thoughts, the process can be speeded up and the necessary elements materialized almost out of time and space. This is what the cooperation between humans and our kingdom can bring about.

PLANTING

Landscape Angel
13 November 1963
It is best to leave each newly prepared bit of land for awhile. In your garden you are almost manufacturing the soil by adding various ingredients. These ingredients, which have been taken out of their accustomed surroundings and transferred into the garden, have their own radiations. They need to settle in and produce a harmonious overall radiation, and we assist in that. We work over the land for you; our work is not just when the plants are added but at all times.

If time is allowed for a good overall radiation to be built up, the plants will not have to contend with many different and perhaps inharmonious wavelengths in the soil.

Landscape Angel
27 April 1967
You ask whether you should contact the deva of each new variety of plant, shrub or tree in the garden. It would be good, it makes humans more real to us. Any contact you make with us in love and understanding helps.

Aubrieta Deva
5 May 1967
There is a store of goodwill from some of us for man; some of us are quite tame. You will find this more in the flowers. You did not find it as much in the vegetables, although they are more cultivated by man than we are. Vegetables are grown to feed man and seldom get appreciation while we are purely decorative and only get appreciation. So we are happily tame while many vegetables are unhappily tame. Yet they are most essential to you humans. Why do you not appreciate them as you do us?

Landscape Angel
16 February 1964
As far as we are concerned, and apart from your considerations such as expense, the more varieties you have in the garden the better. This adds more notes to the orchestra, so to speak. It gives us more scope, introduces more of our world and produces a better balance in the soil. Naturally variety is preferable to one crop. This can be applied to even the smallest unit—the more balanced the mixture, the better.

Rhododendron Deva
21 May 1967
Each species of plants contributes something to the character of the land and changes it. Just as you in your human evolution are now moving out of functioning as separate individuals or separate specialized groups, so the plant world is changing and the flora becoming less specialized and more typical of the whole Earth.

Link with us whenever and wherever you see us. This is good for us and good for our relationship. Notice us, see us with new eyes, notice the way we grow. It will help you to imbibe the unique quality which we bring.

All are part of the whole, but interest lies in the diversity of the parts. The philosophy and the plant life of a country are more related than you might think. Now that greater world unity is coming, let us not lose the essence of each unique contribution.

We thank you for bringing us into the garden; we thank all who have allowed us roothold and life.

Landscape Angel
23 September 1963
It would be much better to grow your own seeds. The whole atmosphere of your garden is different from that of other gardens, and to have the young plants influenced from the beginning and started out with all promise in front of them is important. As with children, the right atmosphere from the early stages develops that which might not otherwise be drawn forth.

Lettuce Deva
29 May 1963
We do not approve of transplanting, for it weakens the plant forces. Nature's method of a prodigious amount of seeds from which only the strong survive ensures the best for the plant. In the best of all worlds, man should sow seeds more thickly than his need and then thin out by

The human mind formulates great hierarchies and ever greater beings, yet the whole truth is simpler still. The truth is within me and within you—the whole of it. Where anything exists, God is. Not part of God but God indivisible.

eliminating those whose life forces he can see are weak. Then he is aiding nature, and in turn nature will produce in health for him.

Landscape Angel
12 October 1963
Our work on the plants connects them up with their surroundings, like a spider's web. Transplanting breaks all that down and we have to start rebuilding in another environment.

Leek Deva
23 April 1964
While it is better for a plant not to be transplanted or moved too often, this is only taking into account the forces of the plant. We know you have other considerations, and every nursery finds it more convenient to move plants for various reasons. We give of our best whatever the conditions, whatever your decisions.

Tibetan Blue Poppy Deva (Meconopsis Baileyi)
16 June 1968
We carry the aura of our native places, a feeling for the environment most natural to us. Man has taken us from our original environment and spread us over the world to adorn his gardens. We are pleased with the appreciation but it is necessary to keep our links with the places that bred us, otherwise we would not be what we are. You take those links and classify them as "shade loving," "acid soil," etc., but those are results. It is the "soul," the overall feel of a place that influences the direction of growth.

We bring with us the aura of what we are. We who are formless and free can breathe that breath of being into a foreign garden and imbue our plants with their native radiations. Let each garden be different and unique, as is each soul. Man's trend should be to unity, not uniformity. Each to his own talent.

OTHER LIFE

The Devas
13 August 1967
It is the fact of oneness which we would emphasize and repeat, because there are many of the one creation which you automatically reject with words like "vermin" or "weeds." These are obvious, but there are many more such rejections in your categories of "good" and "bad" which will change as consciousness grows and expands. We are ever eager to mention this theme of unity to man, it being the immediate step for him to take. We would shout in words of fire that oneness is.

Cornflower Deva
25 July 1967
We like standing together as you have allowed us in the garden rather than our usual way of being scattered throughout a cornfield. Thus we can support one another in our dignity, and the richness of our blue can link up, reflect and multiply.

However, do not think we would not be in the fields, for that too is our place, leavening the ripening grain. Yes, leavening. Your way of growing fields of just one variety is no doubt the simplest for you, but it makes for a preponderance of one note, of one influence, and lacks grace. We add grace and beauty. We interact with other plants and can make up for lacks in soil and atmosphere. We, and others like us, should be allowed to grow where we can, in the conditions that the One Lord makes right for us.

You say that in your neat vegetable rows you cannot have

When you blow your breath on a cold window pane, the frost that appears is part of you, just as the plants we "feed" with our radiations are part of us. We are, in fact, all part of one thing, all different materializations of the one life.

flowers or what are known as weeds. We say you can—not choking the vegetables but mutually giving one to the other. That is a far cry from the way you presently cultivate vegetables, but it is the perfect way and your aim is perfection.

You ask how this can be made practical, a working partnership. The knowledge is right here in our world. For those pioneers who would bring to a garden that amazing perfection in which each plays its part, where there is balance and harmony on all levels, nature's storehouse is available. The signs of this inner knowledge are on the outer plane for all to see and follow up. This should be a new science for man, made easy for him by the cooperation of the nature kingdoms. There are no rigid rules but there are principles: certain plants cooperate best with certain other plants.

God's bounty is limitless and so are his ways. We would share them with you. We of the deva world anticipate this cooperation with the greatest joy and tender our thanks for your ears on this occasion.

Lupin Deva
20 June 1968
We express our thanks to the One Source with each petal and leaf, each color and shape. We are one with the elements, we know it and they know it. We act and interact with no sense of "mine" and "thine," for all the Earth's surface is of one family, one creation, one intelligence.

Can you not sense how all creation shouts for joy that we exist and is just as joyful that our neighbor also exists? We are not as conscious of the moving forces of the insects as we are of other plants, for they are not as close to us. But they cross our path in harmony and we salute them, as we salute you, as having just as much right to life as anything else. We are one under the One. Even if there is what you call a "plague" of some sort, there is a reason for it—usually that man is out of step, doing unnatural things in his separation from the whole.

Landscape Angel
26 September 1963
Plant pests have become unavoidable in the world today. But in your garden we shall avoid them by our very vitality, by ensuring that the plants get everything needed for their physical and spiritual health, by thinking health for them, by allowing no negative thoughts around them, by surrounding and protecting them, by asking specific devas for their advice if necessary. You yourselves have healthy bodies in the world as it is, why not the plants?

Landscape Angel
25 August 1972
An attitude of caring can indeed neutralize or "spiritualize" poisons to a certain extent. But the power of this spiritualization varies, depending upon the positivity of each person. As always it is the motive that matters. Those who refrain from using something they feel would be detrimental to life are helped in other ways. Each must act as he or she is guided from within.

We do not give rules, we encourage and aid growth of consciousness and openness to all life in whatever form it appears.

Blackbird, Starling, Little Birds
14 July 1972
We thank you for the garden which has given us a home where there was no home, a home which is very special to us because of the thoughts and feelings of the humans here.

Yes, we would be glad to show gratitude by more discrimination in what we eat. If you let us know that certain plants are ours, you will see that we adhere to our agreement. Your faith is weak, let us help make it grow.

BEYOND THE PATTERN

Landscape Angel
28 June 1969
Most certainly we will cooperate with you in promoting fast growth or any special development. That is a basic result of the cooperation between our kingdoms. But for far too long man has considered that his intelligence is the only force to deal with situations, forgetting that the Creator has given intelligence to all creatures and that the development and very existence of man is dependent on nature, is nature itself.

Landscape Angel
22 June 1972
We leave entirely to you this question of forcing growth by providing artificial conditions with greenhouses or frames. Always there are pros and cons, always the natural way is more balanced and therefore of better quality. The greenhouse is, of course, invaluable. However, plastic frames, especially if opaque, cut out valuable rays.

Foxglove Deva
14 June 1971
We have told you that the plant patterns are here in our world and that each detail is carried out to perfection. You wonder then why freak growths occur. This is because life is never static; there is always an openness for change, an openness for God's will, a moving onward of life. All creation has an element of experimentation or else it would crystallize.

This is not blind chance. We do it consciously in the moment, as opportunities arise. We cannot instantly change a pattern—it must be done according to natural law—unless, of course, all circumstances are propitious. Here humans can help us and control the circumstances.

Often in the past there has been a great sense of cooperation between a gardener and ourselves in producing some lovely new variety. That sense of cooperation has largely vanished in the world today as man manipulates the plant world for his own selfish purposes, treating it in the same commercial way as he does car components.

You get better results from a child if you use love not force. Although force may bring quicker results, it starts a chain reaction of effects. We are also living things working under the same laws. You have lined us up and forced us to obey, and the chain reaction shows in the upset balance of nature. There is another way to produce change and new varieties and we hope that in this garden, of all places, you will cooperate with us.

Sweet Pea Deva
5 August 1969
I come in like a breath of our perfume, fresh and clear-colored, gay and dainty, not the promise but the fulfillment of the perfection of sweet pea beauty.

Still I wonder that you ask why the flowers do not naturally have long stems. Long stems have been forced by man distorting the natural growth and creating a mutilated unbalanced plant. This is the sort of treatment which causes our kingdom to distrust and move away from the human kingdom. Man has dominion on Earth and there is nothing we can do about his treatment when he considers only his own ends regardless of the means. You cannot expect any of us, particularly those directly concerned with the production of each plant, to feel drawn to humans when we are not permitted the freedom to enjoy unfolding the perfect pattern.

The answer to this problem lies in cooperation, in working together for and with the plan of the whole. You wish long stems in order to arrange the flowers in large groups, and this can be done providing all concerned are working <u>for</u> the project. It can be done not by outer destruction of part of the plant but by inner concentration on the desired development. You humans have a part to play in this because you are the innovators of change.

To ensure our cooperation you have to make clear to and convince our various members that what you are asking is purely motivated and for the good of the whole. Then you must ask, believing, really believing. It should not be an experiment just for the sake of experiment, but always for a useful, productive end, part of the great forward movement of life.

You wonder how to know when we are convinced. Our kingdoms are not unreasonable, but some members are justifiably suspicious. Therefore it would be wise to go slowly until you are proven trustworthy.

With full cooperation between our kingdoms, developments are beyond imagination. We on the devic level would hold a blueprint for that time when all of creation is working together under God for the good of all and there is life-giving harmony between us. We will play our part. Will you play yours?

Wild Rose Deva
30 November 1963
You wonder what connection I have with the hundreds of new varieties of roses developed in the last century. Each variety establishes its own deva as it establishes its type. As a different arrangement of forces is repeated often enough, an entity develops. That entity is like a daughter to

us, yet it is closer than that; it is part of us.

This is difficult to explain to you because you are used to a world of concrete form and separated life, whereas in our worlds all is living, changing force without a sense of separation, without a "self" which individualizes itself from its fellows.

We are rather like a breath, we come and we go. Sometimes joy bubbles up without reason—so do we.

Rose Deva
6 May 1967
You find us beautiful, wise and human-like. Yes, through the ages we and humans have appreciated one another and we have gained certain understandings. You find the way the petals of a rose grow around each other graceful and outstanding. Remember, we are all different, just as each of you is different.

You liken me to a princess in our kingdom, as you cannot find words to express the impression of fine, graceful beauty. That is your classification, not ours; we do not classify. You realize how easily we could be worshipped—do you not have Rose Days in the United States? Yet I also seem retiring.

We are of the angelic ranks. We are of a line of pure servers, and our beauty is expressed in its apartness. Yes, apartness. Some flowers are best in a merry medley; we hold court alone.

The wild roses are my cousins, but I have grown up in the cultivated places with human help, therefore I seem human to you. Remember, I am sort of a shy cousin to all of you as well, and if you claim the relationship, I will come to you. I thank you for your thanks.

THE ELEMENTS

Landscape Angel
7 September 1963
When you think of us, remember that every conceivable part of life is alive, and being alive and manifesting force, there is a spirit of that force.

Rain Deva
10 June 1971
What an integral part of the planet I am—longed for and hated, fierce and gentle, life-giving, changing, one with cloud and sea, linked with wind, nourisher of Earth and refresher even of the morning. Sweeping across the land, I am all this. I am part of all living things, even of your physical self. Yet I am separate

The bridge to heaven
is built with bricks
you make yourself.

and remote, to be placated or persuaded by entreaty, ceremony or modern airplanes.

Can I really leave the wholeness of nature and, regardless of the sun, the wind, and other forces which in unity make up the atmosphere, give or withhold rain? I can—not because I am all-powerful and unique but because you are. You are all these forces in miniature, and depending on your consciousness, you can invoke them. If you are powerful but selfish and not thinking of the whole, what you invoke and receive will be out of balance. But if you desire God's perfection for all, you will invoke and receive that perfection individually and collectively.

If you would rule us, first rule yourself, your own tempestuous nature and arid outlook. Then link with us in love under God, be as fluid as we are and wonders will manifest.

Spirit of the Wind
19 March 1967
You do not know which level is most characteristic of our essence: the soft zephyr, the rollicking gale, the raging cyclone, or something beyond all these. Come deeper, below thought, as in the still center of a cyclone, and imagine our evolution on this Earth. As with your bodies, we are the result of millions of years of evolving patterns. Imagine the effect of an atomic bomb on our volatile media after aeons of ordered perfection.

Yet we are intimate with humans, to whom we bring the breath of life from the Creator. Breathe in that breath in absolute quiet and realize the oneness of life. It is so on the physical level where you depend upon what the Earth produces for breath and food and clothing, and it is so on the higher levels where we are finer, more intelligent expressions of life. Nothing is static, most particularly in our realm of air. Do not try to pin us down, but let us try to understand one another.

Lord of the Elements
6 October 1969
You are a child of the elements, composed of and part of the elements. The world and your bodies were made that you may find and express the joy of the Creator in all his manifestations.

Man is destroying himself because he thinks he is separate. How can you possibly think you are separate? How can you possibly not know that when the wind blows it is part of you, that the sun gives to you and is part of you with each sunbeam, that from the water you came and the water joins you all, that without the air you breathe you could not live? How can you be so dense as not to know that if one suffers, the whole consciousness of the Earth partakes of that? When one rejoices, the whole consciousness knows and is part?

This concept of oneness is being stressed everywhere, being interpreted everywhere. We would emphasize the practical side, the fact that your bodies are one with the environment and that you cannot abuse the Earth without harming yourselves.

Oneness is not just on the high or inner levels where God is but is right here and now. Disturbing the pattern of the Earth, the balance of the seasons, the interplay of all aspects of matter is cutting through the ordained outworking of the One and ruining prospects for the future of man. We must repeat and repeat this, we cannot urge it strongly enough on the mind of man. Do you wonder at the violence of the elements? They will be much more violent unless man picks up and acts on this truth.

Love all of life and so join up with it. Never forget that all of it is part of the Creator and that all of it is also part of you.

REFLECTIONS

Mesembryanthemum Deva

28 June 1968

Throughout the garden, we open ourselves and express our gladness that you finally include us in this conscious contact—in spite of your difficulty with the name we have been given. A long name for a little flower!

It is indeed a matter of rejoicing that the spirit of a flower and the spirit of a human can commune in consciousness, blend and find that one is the other, that there is a real fraternity between our outward manifestations. Whenever we meet we shall now smile secretly within and know without words that there is a bond, that in spite of outward differences, we have been brought together. We do not look to the differences but to the reality and unity of the life within.

When you look at us, perhaps you think, "Pretty little flower, what brilliance of color!" and revel in the beauty. But now you can see all that, with the added knowledge that we are one under the skin, so to speak, and you can open all of yourself to us and we to you. Then do your radiations on all levels come to us, and we have new worlds on which to draw. Then do our nature builders have more bricks with which to build, and you have lost nothing, for the more you empty yourself and share, the more you receive on all levels.

Daffodil Deva

8 April 1971

Everywhere we proclaim the triumphant message of rebirth, of a new season. The air vibrates with this theme. You breathe it in with every breath. Every atom of your body responds.

Life is changing and always new. Just as you are different from what you were a year ago, so is each Spring distinct, a newness to be specifically aware of. Our deva world naturally tunes into this outpouring of energy, because we are the wielders of that energy. It simply comes to us in the rhythm of universal law, the farthest star reflecting oneness with the tiniest substance of Earth as we swing into Spring.

This small planet too is turning into its place of rebirth. Each planet at its appointed time and place responds to and gives from itself a new outburst of life, and this is now your time.

All around you creation reflects the oneness of life, but what of the human mind? We see it caged and colorless, attached to non-essentials or even militant against the progression of life. What a marvel if it were aiding the great energy release of the time, playing its part in fullest expression. What extra joy there will be in Spring when the mind of man joins in!

Our world of energy is offering life new opportunities to be itself. From every daffodil we trumpet a call of new beginnings, of perfection, purity, color, renaissance. Respond, we say; all life is yours. Join us in the oneness of life and with us give eternal thanks to the One.

Lilium Auratum Deva

4 October 1968

We feel it is high time for man to branch out and include in his horizon the different forms of life which are part of his world. He has been forcing his own creations and vibrations on the world without taking into consideration that all living things are part of the whole, just as he is, placed there by divine plan and purpose. Each plant, each mineral has its own contribution to make to the whole, just as each soul has. Man should no longer consider us as lower forms of life with no intelligence and therefore not to be communicated with.

The theory of evolution that puts man at the apex of life on Earth is only correct when viewed from certain angles. It leaves out the fact that God, universal consciousness, is working out the forms of life. For example, according to generally accepted regulations, I am a lowly lily unable to be aware of most things and certainly not able to talk with you. But somehow, somewhere is the intelligence that made us fair and continues to do so, just as somehow, somewhere is the intelligence that produced your intricate physical body.

You are not aware of much of your own inner intelligence and much of your own body is beyond your control. You are conscious of only a certain part of yourself, and likewise you are conscious of only a certain part of the life around you. But you can tune into the greater within and around you. There are vast ranges of consciousness all stemming from the One, the One who is this consciousness in all of us and whose plan it is that all parts of life become more aware of each other and more united in the great forward movement which is life, all life, becoming greater consciousness.

Consider the lily, consider all that it involves, and let us grow in consciousness, unity and love under the One.

Petunia Deva

19 July 1967

We have been wondering when you would get around to us, because we want to say that we love being in this garden. Here we can swirl our forces around in soft rich brilliance in complete comfort. Round and round we go, masters of each little flower, absorbing what the sun gives when it looks at us and what humans give when they look at us; then incorporating that into ourselves.

There is an immense interplay of energy among all creation. As you need air to breathe and fishes need water, so each plant, each part of life, is immersed in an atmosphere that is part of its makeup and to which it also contributes. Man can contribute most of all, and when he does what a wonderful world it will be!

You may, of course, find that we all swirl into as much territory as we can. We would expand and spread and grow, and our neighbor feels the same. Some of us are more rambunctious than others—your job as gardener comes in here!

You are wondering on what level you are contacting us, for we seem so flippant and gay. We have many levels to contact, as do humans. We are alive, we go into life fully. We have to, the season being short. In any case, why hold back when life is there to be expressed? There is nothing to stop us, as there so often seems to be with you.

Go have a look at us. Look at our makeup, become more familiar with it, for it is an expression of us. All is one, all patterns repeat on another level. See how it works.

Good King Henry Deva

24 May 1970

We come, rather squat and not at all colorful, but with our own virtues, definitely a kitchen plant and tenacious in our giving.

Remember, we are a result of aeons of history, perfected in the swirls of time and clearly sounding our useful middle note. You read that we are full of iron and good for the blood, and so it may be from your point of view. We do not have a point of view; we are much too busy being and following our pattern to consider what good we are. This is perhaps just as well, in case we were to become like humans, never content with their lot but always wanting to be as good or better than their neighbors! Comparison seems to us a noxious thing. God made each of us and each of you as we are, to be a particular expression of life.

Yes, I realize now I am comparing. But, you see, I see the beat of each plant and the beat of each human as a rhythm and plan to be complied with, persistent and forever calling out its pattern. And in our adherence to our pattern we wonder how so often you do not comply with yours. We see these magnificent patterns of light that humans have, and we see them covered and ignored. Some of the devas help build your patterns for you and work to keep them pure while, on the whole, you go your way with your real selves unborn, always there to be but never actually being. It is very strange.

Know that each plant has a part to play in the whole or it would not be. We also have a part to play with you. Some of you are more drawn to us than others, but nevertheless it is good for all to partake of a large variety of plants. Your system can select which is most helpful at the time. Of course you could be more selective still and choose exactly which of us are right for you, but few of you take the trouble. If you did, we should probably be more popular!

We continue to sound our unobtrusive note and are here in case of need. So be it, and all thanks to the Maker of all.

Monterrey Cypress Deva

8 May 1967

We come in with a lordly sweep, for we are not just the small trees you see in your garden, but denizens of the magnificent spaces of great hills in the sun and wind. We put up with being hedges, but always in our inner being is this growing toward the open sun-kissed places where we stand out in clustered grandeur. We have our unique portions of Earth's plan to fulfill, yet in this day and age, many of us can only dream of the spaces where we can be fully ourselves.

Man is now becoming controller of the world forests and is beginning to realize how much these are needed by the planet. But he covers acres with one quick-growing species, selecting trees for economic reasons with no awareness at all of the planet's needs. This shows utter ignorance of the purpose of trees and their channeling of diverse forces. The world needs us on a large scale. Perhaps if man were in tune with the infinite, as we are, and were contributing his share, the forces would be in balance. But at present the planet needs more than ever just what is being denied it—the very forces which come through the large and stately trees.

You can just look at a thing,
or you can really "see"
what you are looking at.

ROC

THE NATURE SPIRITS. Some people, possibly more than we realize, talk to the plants in their gardens and houses. Since nobody likes to be made to feel foolish, care is taken not to be caught in the act, and silent rather than voiced speech is used. Is it foolish to talk to plants? They do not move about like animals, and they are inarticulate; but they are alive and, in fact, have a kind of consciousness. People who are sensitive know this and are careful and considerate in the way they handle them.

It is essential to understand the true nature of the plants one cultivates in order to look after and handle them properly. (The word "plant" is used here to include all members of the vegetable kingdom: trees, bushes, flowers, fruits, vegetables and so on.) That plants are sensitive is now becoming a well-known fact. For some years a considerable amount of scientific research has been devoted to demonstrating the reality of this sensitivity. Probably one of the first to study the subject was the remarkable Indian physicist, Sir Jagadis Chandra Bose, who did his work in the early part of this century. For example, he believed that plants suffer severe shock in being transplanted, which delays their establishment in a new place and sets back growth. So before transplanting, he anaesthetized a plant by covering it with a glass bell jar into which he introduced chloroform vapor. Plants treated in this way took at once to their new environment, thus proving his point. The recent work of Cleve Backster and Marcel Vogel in the U.S.A. has demonstrated that plants are sensitive even to human thoughts.

Since the actual facts of these and other investigations now taking place throughout the world are well covered in other publications, there is no need to describe the specifics here. It is what these experiments imply that is vital to us. This does not mean that people with gardens ought, for example, to give trees a shot of anaesthetic before a branch is cut off or that flowers should be offered a whiff of nitrous oxide before being picked. It does mean that plants should be treated with care and consideration and, indeed, with appreciation for the service they give to man.

However, the true nature of plants cannot be described by scientific data only. My experience with the elemental kingdom has demonstrated that to me. But it was only after the research on plant sensitivity was published, opening up a deeper understanding of nature, that I became willing to speak publicly about the experiences I have had with the nature spirits, the elementals.

Their realm is intangible and nonmaterial, and cannot be appreciated by means of the five physical senses, except in a condition of heightened awareness. The existence of the elemental kingdom cannot be proved to the satisfaction of the scientist, nor can the reactions of its inhabitants be demonstrated in the laboratory. Yet to one perceiving with the higher senses, it is as real as any of the more material kingdoms.

When we see the leaves change color in autumn, we might wonder how this is brought about. The botanist has one explanation, based on observation and analysis. The elemental kingdom has another, attributing the work to the energy forms known as fairies and elves. Both are right. It all depends on the way you look at it.

What is meant by the elemental kingdom? Ancient and medieval philosophers believed that all matter was made up of differing combinations of what they called the four "elements"—earth, air, fire and water. They also believed that these elements were inhabited by beings or entities known as "elementals." While earth, air, fire and water are not elements in the present-day meaning of the word, they remain useful concepts in esoteric and occult teachings, because they have a higher significance than the purely physical one. It is important to understand my interpretation of the word "elemental," since certain schools of thought use the word to mean negative or evil entities from the lower astral plane. There are such entities which should preferably be termed "pseudoelementals," since the true elementals come from a higher plane and are part of the angelic hierarchy.

My own contact with such entities, in particular with earth spirits, first took place in the Royal Botanic Gardens of Edinburgh in March, 1966. These gardens, which cover a large area and contain many varieties of bushes, shrubs, flowers and trees, have for years been one of my favorite places. In spite of being mainly a town dweller for all but ten years of my life, I have a great love for nature and, in particular, a deep sense of affinity for trees.

One beautiful afternoon I was wandering about the rock garden and other favorite spots. Eventually I began walking along a path skirting the north side of Inverleith House, which is situated on rising ground in the center of the gardens and is now Edinburgh's Modern Art Gallery. Leaving the path I crossed an expanse of grass, dotted with trees and bushes, to a seat under a tall beech tree. When I sat down I could lean my shoulders and the back of my head against the tree. I became, in some way, identified with this tree, became aware of the movement of the sap in the trunk and even of the infinitely slow growth of the roots. There was a decided heightening of awareness and a sense of expectation. I felt completely awake and full of energy.

Suddenly, I saw a figure dancing round a tree about twenty or twenty-five yards away from me—a beautiful little figure about three feet tall. I saw with astonishment that it was a faun, the Greek mythological being, half human–half animal. He had a pointed chin and ears and two little horns on his forehead. His shaggy legs ended in cloven hooves and his skin was honey-colored. I watched him in astonishment, not believing my eyes.

For a moment I wondered if perhaps he was a boy made up for a school show. Yet he could not be—something about him was decidedly not human. Was he an hallucination? There were one or two other people walking about in the gardens. I looked at them and then back at this beautiful little being. He was still there and seemed to be as solid and real as they were. I tried hard to analyze this experience and explain him away. Suddenly I was brought up sharp—what was I trying to do? Here was a strange and wonderful experience. Why could I not accept it, see what happened and analyze it later? I began to watch the little being with delight as he circled round another tree.

He danced over to where I was sitting, stood looking at me for a moment and then sat cross-legged in front of me. I looked at him. He was very real. I bent forward and said:

"Hallo."

He leapt to his feet, startled, and stared at me.

Can you see me?

"Yes."

I don't believe it. Humans can't see us.

"Oh, yes. Some of us can."

What am I like?

I described him as I saw him. Still looking bewildered, he began to dance round in small circles.

What am I doing?

I told him.

He stopped dancing and said, *You must be seeing me.*

He danced across to the seat beside me, sat down and, turning towards me, looked up and said, *Why are human beings so stupid?*

In some ways I may be over-personalizing this being. I realize I was not seeing him with my physical sight, though when I closed my eyes he was not there. And the communication between us was, no doubt, taking place on a mental or telepathic level by means of thought transference, probably in the form of images and symbols projected into my unconscious mind and

translated into words by my consciousness. However, I cannot be certain whether I was speaking to him mentally or aloud. (Now, when I meet such beings, I usually speak aloud.) I have to report our exchanges in the form of dialogue, since that is what I hear in my head. I am aware that in a case like this there is always the possibility of coloration from my own mind. However, applying my training as a scientist in objective observation and analysis, I do try to report experiments and experiences as accurately as possible.

To return to his question of why human beings are so stupid, I asked him, "In what way stupid?"

In many ways. What were the strange skins or coverings they had, some of which could be taken off? Why did they not go about in the natural state as he did? I told him the skins were called clothes and that we wore them for protection and for warmth and because it was not considered right to be without them. This latter he could not understand, so I did not pursue the subject. We talked about houses, and motor cars which seemed to him to be boxes on wheels in which human beings dashed about, sometimes bumping into each other. Was it a game? he wanted to know.

He told me he lived in the Gardens. This is a partial truth, as he is an inhabitant of another plane of existence as well. His work was to help the growth of trees. He also told me that many of the nature spirits have lost interest in the human race, since they have been made to feel that they are neither believed in nor wanted.

If you humans think you can get along without us, just try!

"Some of us do believe in you and want your help. I do, for one."

The wonderful thing for me in this meeting was the sense of companionship. I felt an amazing harmony with this wonderful little being sitting beside me. A communication was taking place between us that did not need to be put into words. We sat for some time without speaking. Eventually I rose and said I must return home.

Call me when you return here and I will come to you.

He told me his name was Kurmos. I asked him if he could visit me.

Yes, if you invite me.

"I do. I shall be delighted if you will come and visit me."

You do believe in me?

"Yes, of course I do."

And you like us?

"Yes, I have much affection for the nature spirits." This was true, though he was the first one I had actually seen.

Then I'll come now.

On the way through the streets of Edinburgh to my home, I was amused to think of the sensation it might have caused had this strange, delightful little faun been as visible to the passers-by as he was to me.

We entered my flat. I have a fairly large collection of books and my two main rooms are lined with book shelves. Kurmos showed great interest. What were they and why so many? I explained to him that they contained facts, ideas, speculations and theories, accounts of past events, stories invented by the writers and so on, all of which were written down, put into print and made up into books which could be read by others. His comment was:

Why? You can get all the knowledge you want by simply wanting it.

I told him human beings could not do that very wonderful thing—at least not yet. We had to be content to get our facts and knowledge from other people or from books.

Again we sat for some time in silence and contented harmony. Then he got up; it was time for him to return to the Gardens. The door of the room was open, and he walked out into the hall. I followed him and, probably because he looked so solid and real, I opened the door onto the landing. He passed me and ran lightly down the stairs. As he reached the bottom step, he faded out.

This was an astonishing experience, one which I am certain I could not have imagined. My imagination works on the prosaic and practical levels and is not inclined to fantasy. And why a faun? That puzzled me. I had read no Greek mythology for years.

The next time I went to the Gardens I called to him, as he had told me to do, and he was immediately by my side. Again we sat together in silence. Though I knew that here was infinite, mature wisdom combined with the naivety of a child, I did not want to ask him questions; the wonderful harmony and companionship were enough. I intuitively felt that what was right for me to know regarding him would be given at the appropriate time.

I did not know then that these meetings with Kurmos were leading me to something even more unusual which was to take place over a month later, at the end of April. One evening I had been visiting friends who lived on the south side of Edinburgh. It was after eleven o'clock and I was walking home.

Few people were about, and I thought how peaceful the city was at the moment. I walked down Princes Street, Edinburgh's main thoroughfare. As I turned the corner onto the street which runs alongside the National Gallery, I stepped

into an extraordinary "atmosphere." I had never before encountered anything quite like it. While it is difficult to describe, I might say it was as if I had no clothes on and was walking through a medium denser than air but not as dense as water. I could feel it against my body. It produced a sensation of warmth and tingling like a mixture of pins and needles and an electric shock. This was accompanied by a heightened awareness and the same feeling of expectation I had had in the Gardens before meeting Kurmos.

Then I realized that I was not alone. A figure—taller than myself—was walking beside me. It was a faun, radiating a tremendous power. I glanced at him. Surely this was not my little faun grown up suddenly? We walked on. He turned and looked at me.

Well, aren't you afraid of me?

"No."

Why not? All human beings are afraid of me.

"I feel no evil in your presence. I see no reason why you should want to harm me. I do not feel afraid."

Do you know who I am?

I did at that moment. "You are the great god Pan."

Then you ought to be afraid. Your word "panic" comes from the fear my presence causes.

"Not always. I am not afraid."

Can you give me a reason?

"It may be because of my feeling of affinity with your subjects, the earth spirits and woodland creatures."

You believe in my subjects?

"Yes."

Do you love my subjects?

"Yes, I do."

In that case, do you love me?

"Why not?"

<u>Do you love me?</u>

"Yes."

He looked at me with a strange smile and a glint in his eyes. He had deep, mysterious brown eyes.

You know, of course, that I'm the devil? You have just said you love the devil.

"No, you are not the devil. You are the god of the woodlands and the countryside. There is no evil in you. You are Pan."

Did the early Christian Church not take me as a model for the devil? Look at my cloven hooves, my shaggy legs and the horns on my forehead.

"The Church turned all pagan gods and spirits into devils, fiends and imps."

Was the Church wrong then?

"The Church did it with the best intentions from its own point of view. But it was wrong. The ancient gods are not necessarily devils."

We crossed Princes Street and turned a corner. He turned to me:

What do I smell like?

Since he had joined me I had been aware of a wonderful scent of pine woods, of damp leaves, of newly turned earth and of woodland flowers. I told him.

Don't I smell rank, like a goat?

"No, you don't. There is a faint, musk-like smell, like the fur of a healthy cat. It is pleasant—almost like incense. Are you still claiming to be the devil?"

I have to find out what you think of me. It's important.

"Why?"

For a reason.

"Won't you tell me what it is?"

Not now. It will become apparent in time.

We walked on. Pan was walking very close beside me.

You don't mind me walking beside you?

"Not in the least."

He put his arm round my shoulder. I felt the actual physical contact.

You don't mind if I touch you?

"No."

You really feel no repulsion or fear?

"None."

Excellent.

I could not think why he was making this determined effort to produce a sign of fear. I am not claiming to be a brave man; there are many things that would scare me out of my life. But, for some reason or other, I felt no fear of this being. Awe, because of his power, but not fear—only love.

I asked him where his pan-pipes were. He smiled at the question:

I do have them, you know.

And there he was, holding them between his hands. He began to play a curious melody. I had

heard it in woods before and I have often heard it since, but it is so elusive that so far I have been unable to remember it afterwards.

When we reached the downstairs main door of the house where I live, he disappeared. I had a strong feeling, however, that he was still with me when I went in.

I had no idea why this strange encounter had happened, or why this being had chosen to show himself to me. It looked as if the meeting with the little faun in the Botanic Gardens had been a preliminary step in bringing it about, and I was feeling reasonably certain that neither of these beings was imaginary. I wondered what was going to happen next.

As a child I had passionately believed in fairies and loved both the Greek myths and their Norse equivalents, whose gods were very real to me. The Pan I knew was the wonderful and beautiful being in the chapter "The Piper at the Gates of Dawn" in Kenneth Grahame's *The Wind in the Willows.* Over a period of time these feelings were suppressed by school life and replaced by an irrepressible curiosity to find out how and why things worked, eventually becoming almost an obsessional interest in physics and chemistry.

By the time I reached my early thirties, the chronic heart ailment which had prevented me from ever having a steady job had come to a critical point, and I was strongly advised to retire to an atmosphere of complete quiet. For ten years I lived in comparative isolation in the country, pursuing my interests in science and literature, and developing a close contact with nature. Despite my interest in esoteric and occult subjects, I was unaware of the existence of such beings as nature spirits the entire time I lived there. I would certainly have dismissed belief in the real existence of fairies, gnomes and elves as superstition, figments of the imagination. In fact, even after I did make contact with Pan and the world of the nature spirits, I went through a period of time when I doubted their existence, when it seemed to me that the whole thing might be a fantasy, the projection of a part of my own unconscious mind. In time I realized that the nature spirits had shown themselves to me for a specific reason.

This became clear when I met Pan again in early May, 1966 on Iona, a tiny island of the Inner Hebrides which is considered to be an ancient center of spiritual power. Peter Caddy and I were standing in the Hermit's Cell, a ring of stones which

is all that is left of the place where St. Columba used to go in retreat. In front of us was a gentle grassy slope which hid from sight the Iona Abbey on the other side of the island. I became aware of a large figure lying in the ground there. I could see him through the grass. It appeared to be a monk in a brown habit with the hood pulled over the head so

that the features were concealed. His feet were towards the cell. As I watched, he raised his hands and rolled back the hood. It was Pan. He rose up out of the ground and stood facing us. He smiled and said:

I am the servant of Almighty God, and I and my subjects are willing to come to the aid of mankind, in spite of the way he has treated us and abused nature, if he affirms belief in us and asks for our help.

Here was a step towards the reconciliation of Pan and the world of the nature spirits with man. Because I had been able to respond to him without fear, Pan could communicate with me and use me as a mediator between man and nature. This does not make me important in myself—I am simply a channel for this work.

Vital to this reconciliation is the recognition of Pan's true nature. He is a great being, the god of the whole elemental kingdom as well as of the animal, vegetable and mineral kingdoms. People may feel uneasy in his presence because of the awe he inspires, but there ought to be no fear.

All human beings are afraid of me, he had said at our first meeting, not as a threat but with sadness. *Did the early Christian Church not take me as a model for the devil?* That is why Pan is feared—because of the image projected onto him. This stigma must be lifted in order to reestablish the true link between man and nature.

Pan has said he would prefer not to be represented in any material form at all. Yet, if he must be, he insists on being accepted, in our culture, as the Greek myth depicts him, half human–half animal. There is a fitness about it in its symbolism. The human upper half represents intellect, united with a powerful, mysterious,deep energy represented by the animal lower half—an energy not yet revealed in man. It is important to consider Pan and the nature spirits in their own right when they take on these human-like forms and not compare them with our own conception of human beauty. Some people assume that Pan must be ugly. This is far from the case. In his own right he is one of the most beautiful beings I have ever seen. Only the horns on the forehead, the cloven hooves and the fine silky hair on the legs suggest the animal part. The legs are human, not animal.

It is very important to realize that though Pan can appear in such a form, he is *not* a being restricted to one place. The word "pan" means "all," "everywhere." Pan is a universal energy, a cosmic energy, which is constantly found throughout the whole of nature. He could appear personified in many different places at the same time and should never be thought of as restricted to a corner of the garden or sitting on a hilltop beside a gorse bush.

It may be helpful to consider why Pan and the nature spirits assume such forms. Their primary state is what may be termed a "light body." It is a whirl or vortex of energy in constant motion. Nebulous like a fine mist, it glows with colored light, sometimes one single color, sometimes two or more which do not mix but remain separate like the colors of a rainbow. It frequently changes color and is often covered with a multitude of fine curved lines. These are usually golden but can be other colors. They appear to flow like liquid in a pipe, forming continually changing patterns of incredible beauty. These light bodies differ from each other in size and brilliancy, varying from pastel shades to strong, bright colors. All are beautiful, pure and luminous, glowing with inward radiance. They may be regarded as whirls of energy, but energy with intelligence. It is possible to see and to communicate with these light bodies.

However, the elementals or nature spirits cannot carry out their work with plants in these pure bodies. In this work they use the energies channeled to them by the devas to build up an "etheric body" or "etheric counterpart" for each plant, according to its archetypal pattern. The plant grows and develops within this counterpart. In order to fulfill their task, the nature spirits too must take on an etheric body.

In esoteric knowledge, the etheric plane is made up of a fine energy substance from which is

created the mold for every form we see manifest on the physical plane. Each material form has an etheric counterpart. That such a thing exists at all will be questioned by many people. At the moment it cannot be scientifically proven, though no doubt this will be possible in the future.

We do know ourselves to be far more than just our physical bodies. According to esoterics, we have an etheric body, as well as other higher bodies. We are incarnate spirit. So too, do plants have at least etheric bodies, if not higher ones as well. This is why man must be careful when he interferes with the natural growth of plants. In trying to alter the form through artificial means, often using force, man can depart from the archetypal design. Apart from the fear and pain produced in the plant, this can bring about lack of alignment with the etheric counterpart, causing further discomfort and distress.

Rather than using force to bring about changes in plants, it would be much better if man would ask the nature spirits to bring them about by modifying the etheric counterpart. This they will do if they are convinced that the change is reasonable and a help to mankind, not simply for expediency. At the moment, they are limited in their actions by the general disbelief in their power and even in their existence.

What of the etheric bodies of the nature spirits themselves? In his myths, legends and fairy tales, man has depicted a vast gallery of what he has referred to as "supernatural" beings. (Actually, "paraphysical" would be a more accurate word to describe them.) To what extent the etheric forms of these beings were the product of man's own creative imagination or the result of inspiration from an outside source is difficult to determine.

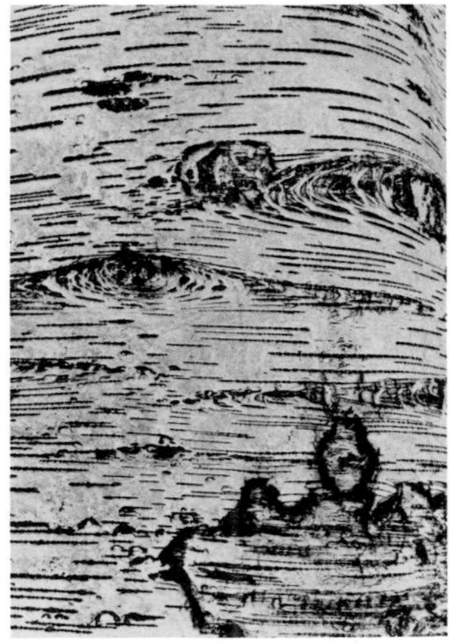

Suffice it to say that there exists what one might call a vast reservoir of "thought forms" produced by the existence and persistence of these tales. Often thought about and talked about, these forms have been preserved both orally and in print. Thus, an elemental entity wishing to assume a body can "put on" any of these thought forms and appear personified as that particular being—Greek or Norse god, elf, gnome, faun, fairy and so on. In myths and legends these paraphysical beings have been depicted in a human form and as behaving in a human manner. Of course, they are essentially formless and only adopt a form and its characteristic behavior when needed.

In September of 1966, I had an encounter with Pan that was to bring me a deeper understanding of his form and nature. I had attended a weekend course conducted by Sir George Trevelyan at Attingham Park. Before leaving on Monday morning, I was prompted to go to an area known as The Mile Walk on Attingham's extensive and beautiful grounds. I followed the path until I came to the Rhododendron Walk which is considered by some to be a place of great spiritual power. At its entrance is a huge cedar tree with a bench beneath it. I sat there for some time, enjoying the beauty of the place, then rose and entered the Walk. As I did so, I felt a great build-up of power and a vast increase in awareness. Colors and forms became more significant. I was aware of every single leaf on the bushes and trees, of every blade of grass on the path standing out with startling clarity. It was as if physical reality had become much more real than it normally is, and the three-dimensional effect we are used to had become even more solid. This kind of experience is nearly impossible to describe in words. I had the impression of complete reality, and all that lies within and beyond it felt immediately imminent. There was an acute feeling of being one with nature in a complete way, as well as being one with the Divine, which produced great exultation, and a deep sense of awe and wonder.

I became aware of Pan walking by my side and of a strong bond between us. He stepped behind me and then walked into me so that we became one, and I saw the surroundings through his eyes. At the same time, part of me—the recording, observing part—stood aside. The experience was not a form of possession but of identification, a kind of integration.

The moment he stepped into me the woods became alive with myriad beings—elementals, nymphs, dryads, fauns, elves, gnomes, fairies and so on, far too numerous to catalogue. They varied in size from tiny little beings a fraction of an inch in height—like the ones I saw swarming about on a clump of toadstools—to beautiful elfin creatures, three or four feet tall. Some of them danced round me in a ring; all were welcoming and full of rejoicing. The nature spirits love and delight in the work they do and express this in movement.

I felt as if I were outside time and space. Everything was happening in the now. It is impossible to give more than a faint impression of the actuality of this experience, but I would stress the exultation and the feeling of joy and delight. Yet, there was an underlying peace, contentment and a sense of spiritual presence.

I found myself in a clearing at the end of this part of the Rhododendron Walk, where there is a great oak tree. I turned and walked back the way I had come. I now had pan-pipes in my hands and was aware of shaggy legs and cloven hooves. I began to dance down the path, playing on the pipes—the melody I had heard Pan play. The numerous birds responded, their songs making an exquisite counterpoint to the music of the pipes. All the nature beings were active, many dancing as they worked.

When I had almost reached the spot where the experience had started, the heightened awareness began to fade and Pan withdrew, leaving me once more my ordinary self. I stopped dancing and walked on. The pan-pipes had gone.

The change from this strange ecstatic experience to the normal reality of everyday life was not a disappointment. What I had experienced was still there; it is always there, for it is a part of the true reality. Because of our dulled senses and our habit of going through life wearing materialistic blinkers in a condition verging on sleepwalking, we are unaware of the fantastic beauty of the life around us. Of course, it would not do if we were aware of it all the time; that would be too overwhelming and make us incapable of performing our daily tasks. However, we could well be more aware of our surroundings without carrying it that far.

Approaching the end of the path and the cedar tree, I began to walk sedately, which was just as well since a boy was sitting on the seat nearby. It might have been disconcerting for at least one of us if I had come dancing down the path playing invisible pipes at my age.

Several weeks later I again had this experience of becoming one with Pan. It happened in St. Annes-on-Sea where I had gone with several friends who were attending a conference. I was walking alone in the garden across from the meeting place when I became aware of Pan standing beside me. As before, he stepped into me. This "compound being," as it might be called, summoned the nature spirits together to help in what was to take place. The pond and all the bushes and trees became immediately alive with beings of many different kinds. I—or should I say "we"—walked onto a raised part of the gardens from which it was possible to look across to the house where the meeting was taking place. Pan within me called upon the green ray of the nature forces to rise up through the house. Slowly this light rose until it emerged from the roof. After some time, Pan withdrew.

I left the garden and about five minutes later met Peter Caddy who had just come from the house. He startled me by saying that Pan had been in the room and communicated with a certain woman present there who was a sensitive and that, of the fifteen others present in the room, nearly all had had visions or impressions connected with nature.

The significance of these two episodes became clearer in time. We are told to turn within, to seek God within, to seek Christ within. But this withinness is not contained in my physical body which would limit it; it is in all dimensions of space and time; it is infinite, the eternal now. We turn away from the outside world, the material world which so many believe to be the only reality, to seek that true reality which is within and yet everywhere.

In that sense, Pan is within me, the whole universe is within me, the elemental kingdom, the angelic hierarchy, God himself is within me. This withinness is the All, the great mystery which we poor humans cannot hope to understand completely. We can only grope toward it and in some way seek to apprehend it.

I had often wondered about the process that lay behind these experiences of heightened awareness that permit a glimpse into true reality. In particular, I was interested in knowing how my ability to perceive nature spirits had come about. Certainly, to my knowledge, I hadn't asked for it. In 1972 I had an encounter with Pan that answered some of these questions.

I had gone to the Botanic Gardens in the early afternoon of Midsummer's Eve, a very important day for the nature spirits. From the moment I entered the heath garden, it was alive with myriad beings. Green elves, three to four feet tall, were walking in front of me, full of joy and delight, and little gnomes were running about almost under my feet. The beautiful little faun Kurmos came towards me from among the bushes. Greeting me with joy, he danced off between the elves.

I walked to the top of the heath garden towards a certain tree of the species *Zelkova Carpinifolia* which has been referred to as the "Tree of Life" by Richard St. Barbe Baker. I like to greet this strange tree whenever I go to the garden. This time my attention was caught by a group of markings on the bark that were in the form of a figure about fourteen inches high. I had never noticed this effect before. The figure was distinct. It was strange and slightly sinister—a faun-like being with longish straight horns; the eyes were quite noticeable. I had been aware of the tree spirit but had never seen it before. Was this a representation of it on the bark? A mist formed between me and the tree, and I found myself looking at the entity itself, standing in front of the tree. He was about my own height, thickset and dark-skinned. His fierce eyes challenged me.

Will you touch the tree as you have always done, aware this time that you are doing it through me?

I laid my hand on the trunk of the tree and felt the usual strong flow of energy.

You find me odd—not what you expected. You are not repulsed?

"I am disconcerted. You certainly are not what I expected, but I love this tree, and you are the tree. You are not evil."

I am neither good nor evil. My tree has been called the Tree of Life. I am what you make of me.

I moved away from the tree and turned around. Pan was beside me. He asked if seeing this aspect of the tree spirit had made a difference in how I felt about the tree.

"No. The energy field of the tree is unchanged." I looked at Pan enquiringly. "You said, 'this aspect of the tree spirit,' meaning he has others?"

Yes, he has others. The form in which he shows himself is suited to the occasion. It has a purpose.

"To test my reaction? Or to disconcert me?"

Pan smiled. *Perhaps a bit of both.*

I proceeded along a path toward an empty bench. Kurmos, who had been watching, came and sat beside me.

"This reminds me of our first meeting when you asked why human beings are so stupid."

Kurmos looked up at me. *We find human behavior amusing at times, but so often it is destructive, cruel and horrible, or so it appears to us. We try to understand but it isn't easy. We know there are those who love nature, who love this garden. No doubt they would love us if they could see us. This makes us happy and we draw near to them. Some of them may even be aware of us, though they cannot see us. Why can you see us so clearly?*

"I suppose I am a privileged person, one of those chosen to link with Pan and help to renew the old contact between mankind and the nature spirits."

Pan appeared that moment standing opposite us.

You were chosen because you are suited to the task. Your entire life has been a training and preparation for this. As soon as the integration between your lower self and your higher self reached a certain degree of completion you were bound to see us. Your lower self and your physical body had to be trained and conditioned for many years before this level could be reached.

Because of your makeup and the work you have to do, you see me and my subjects as if we were part of the material world. This is not your projection, it is bringing cosmic reality into manifestation when it is right to do so.

"Can you explain the mechanism?" I asked. "I am certain it is not due to heightened sensitivity of physical sight only."

It is a mixture of that plus an added higher vision brought about by the development of cosmic consciousness.

"That makes sense to me. But I am unable to control it myself. For instance, I cannot wish to see a nature spirit and immediately do so, however hard I try."

It is done from our side—when it is right for you to have this heightened vision or when a particular entity wishes to become visible to you.

"How is that done?"

Imagine a theatre with a large stage. The stage is in darkness. It is thronged with people but you cannot see them because of the darkness, which symbolizes your lack of sensitivity. A narrow-beam spotlight picks out one of them and he immediately becomes visible in this way. Similarly, lights could pick out a group or the whole stage could be lit. The light symbolizes your heightened senses. It is a rough analogy but it may answer your question.

"It does. The lights are controlled by some being on your side, I take it?"

Yes.

"Therefore, I can't select the entities I am to see or when. But I am aware of and can communicate with your subjects."

Of course, you can do this at any time though you may only be able to see us on special occasions. The moment you think of an entity you are in immediate communication with it. You may or may not be aware of the response, according to your degree of sensitivity at the time, but it will almost certainly be there.

"Can anyone make such a contact?"

Yes, anyone can and it is important that this should be understood. The one-way contact is always there, but being aware of the response usually needs training or at least practice. It is very subtle and easily missed.

"There are many who would genuinely and sincerely like to share my experiences and I am frequently asked how they can set about it."

And you hedge and say, "Some day you probably will if your faith is strong enough. Don't try too hard, it will just happen at the unexpected

moment." You also tell them to follow your example and live in comparative isolation in the country for ten years, as you did yourself.

"I do, and most of them look aghast and say they could not possibly do that; they haven't the time and it might mean giving up too much."

There is always time for the important things. Communicating with my subjects is not a garden game for the odd half hour when there is nothing else to do. I have observed far too much of this contemptuous superior attitude of man towards my subjects; it is almost worse than disbelief. Leave it at that and let's return to the genuine people who are legitimately curious about my world and would dearly love to see us. There is nothing wrong with that except that it very rarely works—they try too hard.

Perhaps this is fortunate as they do not realize how dangerous it might be if their desire was granted too soon, before either their bodies or their minds had been prepared and conditioned for the experience and the right degree of cosmic consciousness had been reached.

Many people who believe in the nature spirits and love them can be aware of them, can communicate and sometimes even see them in brief glimpses. With such people they will always cooperate when invoked, which simply means asking for help. This simple awareness is open to anyone who seeks it. It is this total link that must be initiated from our side when it is required.

Certainly a reconciliation between man and the nature spirits is now required for the survival of the world. For this reason Pan had to initiate a direct contact. As I see it, the main reason for my communication with the elementals was the contribution it made to the work of the Findhorn garden. By bringing onto a conscious level the links already existing there with nature spirits, I could receive guidance and knowledge complementary to Dorothy's link with the devic world. Thus, the aim of the Findhorn garden of full cooperation among the three kingdoms—the devas, the nature spirits and man—could be established and built up.

It is vital for the future of mankind that belief in the nature spirits and their god Pan is reestablished

and that they are seen in their true light. In spite of the outrages man has committed against nature, these beings are only too pleased to help him if he will seek and ask for their cooperation.

Once Pan had told me that, although I had been chosen by him, I had actually started the contact myself. I was immensely curious to know what he meant. In the autumn of 1974, I believe I found out.

Some years ago, on the grounds of a large estate near the little seaside town of Rosemarkie in north Scotland, there existed an enchanting place known as the Fairy Glen. In 1903 when I was approaching my fourth birthday, my parents brought me there. I have vivid memories of a waterfall with two streams of water, a flight of earthen steps, a bridge over a stream and, above all, a wishing well with a pebbly bottom under an overhanging rock. In 1974 I had gone back with a friend to visit this place. We found the wishing well completely filled in, but the waterfall, splashing down into a rocky pool, was still there. It was a lovely day, and we sat looking at the falling water and enjoying the feel of the place.

Suddenly three little gnomes appeared on a flat rock in front of me.

My, you have grown up, said one of them.

"What do you mean?"

We remember a little boy coming here long ago in your time, piped in the second gnome.

It was you and aren't you glad your wish was granted? asked the third.

"What wish?"

Don't you remember dropping a penny in the wishing well and wishing you could see fairies and talk with them? the first gnome asked.

And bubbles rose from the pebbles on the bottom

of the well, which meant that your wish would be granted, added the second.

I certainly did drop pennies in the well and make wishes. I cannot say I remember that specific one, but it is very likely true, for I believed in fairies then as I do once more today. So that could be how it all began and why it happened to me.

To anyone who may have expressed a wish to see and talk with nature spirits, whether or not you have dropped a penny into a wishing well, remember it took sixty-three years for my wish to be granted, and don't lose hope. The nature spirits must be believed in with complete sincerity and faith. They must be appreciated and given thanks and love for the work they do. Let us try in our own ways to make friends with these wonderful beings and ask their help in making Earth a beautiful and perfect place.

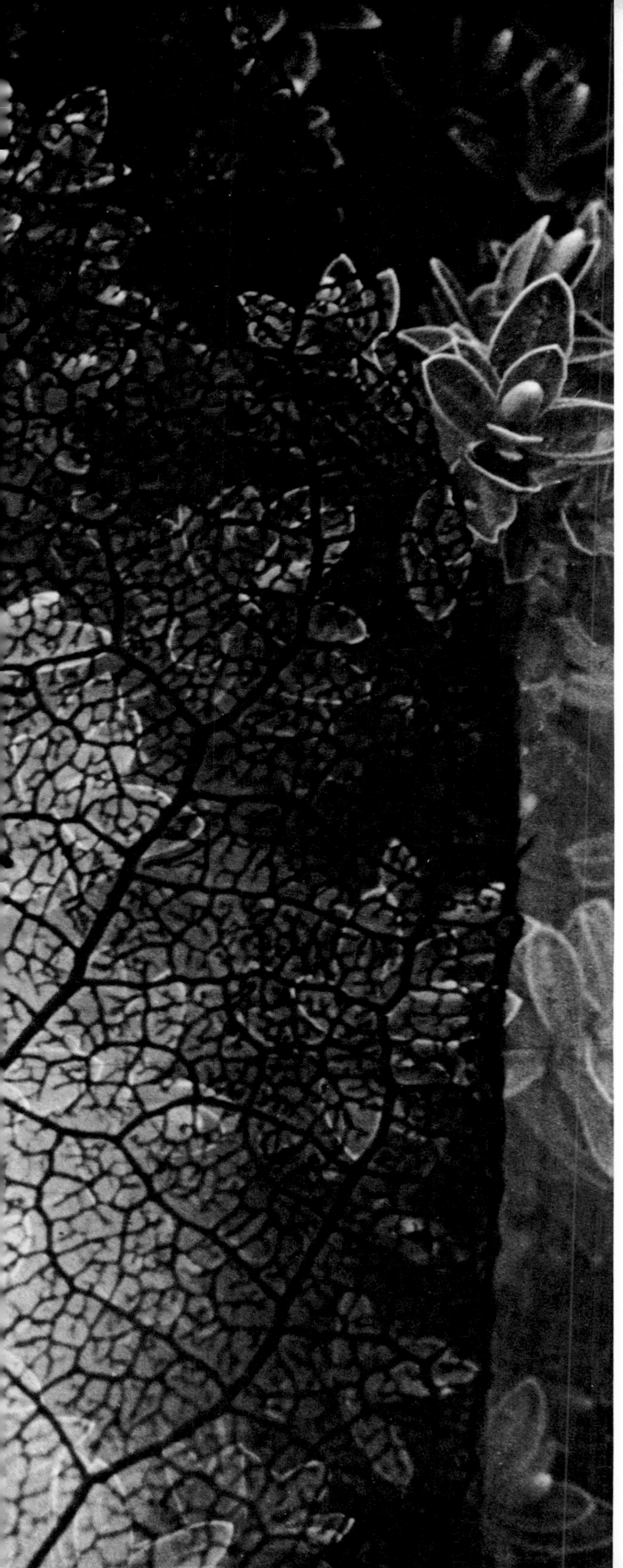

We have not only to cooperate with the nature kingdoms, but we have to allow them to become one with us. Through this marriage, we are more truly human.

DAVID

FROM DOMINANCE TO SYNTHESIS. Like so many people, my first contact with Findhorn was through the story of its garden. By January of 1969, I was beginning my fifth year of work in America as a lecturer and educator in spiritual and esoteric themes. A new age, based on an awareness of the oneness of all life and the creative divinity inherent in that life, was taking form within us and about us. This perception had grown so strong in me that it demanded a commitment of action. I withdrew from a university study program in biochemistry and began a career of sharing with other people the insights that were filling my consciousness.

On one level, with the help of my colleague and companion, Myrtle Glines, I was very successful in this new venture. My field of lecturing covered a large area of the western United States, and I usually had at least four classes going a week in addition to a busy counselling program. On the other hand, I found that simply lecturing about the New Age and the birth of a new consciousness was not sufficient. I was contributing to an ever-swelling river of words coming from lecturers and writers around the world; but words alone, no matter how lofty, would not suffice to bring the new world into being. Something more than study groups meeting once a week was needed—something to demonstrate these concepts and principles in action, to prove that the theories really worked and were practical contributions to modern life.

This quest for "something more" led me into creating workshops based on performing arts techniques and into investigating small local communities begun by groups of young people in the San Francisco area where Myrtle and I were working. I was also trying to learn what groups were doing in other parts of the world. In January of 1969, a colleague told me about a small community in northern Scotland, growing a miracle garden on sand through communication with devas, elves and other nature spirits. He showed me an advance copy of their booklet entitled *The Findhorn Garden, An Experiment in the Cooperation Between Three Kingdoms.* I was enthralled. Here was the very thing I had been looking for, a living demonstration of a trans-physical reality, anchored in tangible manifestation.

The impact this story had on me transcended the phenomenal aspects, such as extraordinarily large vegetables or even the vitality of the plants growing on sand. The greatest significance lay in the practical demonstration of a spiritual solution to the developing world crisis in ecology and pollution, as well as food production. Clearly the current ecology movement is attempting to restore balance by pointing out the interrelatedness of life upon the Earth, insisting upon a holistic vision for survival. However, most ecological presentations still portray nature solely in its form aspects. If humanity is to survive, they rightfully proclaim, the environment must be kept in balance. Little, if anything, is said about the relationship between humanity and nature as two aspects of a single life, or the soul relationship between them. But here was the Findhorn garden, demonstrating a solution based on that same oneness of life that had become a guiding principle for me, and on an expanded vision of environment which included levels of consciousness not ordinarily taken into account.

It was a year and a half before the way opened for Myrtle and me to visit Findhorn. I shall never forget that June day in 1970 when we arrived at the community and saw the garden for the first time. Brilliantly beautiful flowers surrounded trim, neat bungalows and caravans: color, life, fragrance, vitality and form synthesized into a dynamic wholeness. It was less an experience of seeing than of being; of being embraced into a fellowship of growth and blooming and having one's human potentials affirmed and blended into a larger

whole in which everything could find fulfillment. Here was a garden, to be sure, but its "gardenness" did not stop with the plants. The garden was everything and everyone.

In the three years that followed, before Myrtle and I left to pick up our work in the United States and elsewhere, we witnessed the translation of this garden potential and its energy of all-embracing growth and life affirmation into many activities which outwardly bore little resemblance to horticulture. Soon the community had expanded into areas such as arts and crafts, printing and publishing, construction, communications and a college program—all in addition to the work in the garden. Yet, all these activities bore the stamp of the organic energies that had been so well anchored in the garden demonstration.

The role of Findhorn, since its inception, has been to demonstrate communion and cooperation with nature, based on a vision of the life and purposeful intelligence inherent in it. This is an important role, considering that it arises within a Western cultural milieu in which nature has been increasingly quantified as part of an industrial process. "Nature" has become equated with a set of statistics defining the resources, conditions and projections that enter into the equations of growth and progress. Nature has become a commodity to be used and exploited, an adversary to be conquered and dominated.

The archetypal paradigm lying behind so much of the motivation and action of Western civilization has been that of man created in the image of God and given dominion over all the Earth, even as God has dominion. In the Hebraic-Christian tradition

this is most clearly expressed in Genesis 1:26-28:
And God said, Let us make man in our image, after our likeness: and let him have dominion over the fish of the sea, and over the fowl of the air, and over the cattle, and over all the earth, and over every creeping thing that creepeth upon the earth. So God created man in his own image, in the image of God created he him: male and female created he them. And God blessed them, and God said unto them, Be fruitful and multiply, and replenish the earth and subdue it; and have dominion over the fish of the sea, and over the fowl of the air, and over every living thing that moveth upon the earth.

Without understanding the true significance of this reference, we have succeeded to a considerable degree in fulfilling this archetype on the physical level. The Earth and all its lives lie subdued before our technological strengths and processes, unreplenished. The concept of a spirit, an intelligence, a god moving within nature and ordering all its aspects, has been dismissed as myth and legend of simpler cultures. It is Findhorn's role to bring the mythology to life again.

This idea of a life and spirit informing nature and directing its activities is not new within human culture; it is the basis for such philosophies as animism and pantheism. The most sacred esoteric teachings throughout the ages have held that in understanding the inner and outer realities of nature, humanity can understand itself, and vice versa. In our time, we are gaining new insights into the nature of identity itself and into processes for self-revelation. Out of this exploration comes an opportunity to reinvestigate and to restate the characteristics of the inner nature behind the outer environment and its forms. We have an opportunity to step beyond the symbols, legends and mythologies that have tried to express these inner realities, to go beyond the fairy stories of our childhoods, and begin to understand what these images were meant to convey. In so doing, we cannot help but understand ourselves and our processes of unfoldment more deeply. Such an understanding is the hoped-for foundation for a new relationship between humanity and a world that will be transforming and highly creative, unfolding a planetary Eden for the benefit and growth of all forms of life. Findhorn is a strategy of exploration into the nature of that understanding and relationship.

In the course of its development—indeed, from its outset—Findhorn has pursued this exploration through communication with the inner reality behind the forms of nature, combined with practical action within the garden as a result of these communications. The community is demonstrating that there do exist lives from other dimensions of energy who are directly responsible for the manifestation of nature—the invisible lords and builders of the environment, known as the devas and the elementals. The story of the Findhorn garden related in this book is essentially the story of communication with these beings and the resulting manifestation within the garden.

While living in the community, I became involved in this process of communication. The existence of realms of life and energy beyond the physical had been a reality for me since I was a very young child, and I had had some previous experience of communicating with nature spirits before I came to Findhorn. However, since others such as Roc and Dorothy were the usual sources of specific information and were in many ways more attuned to the garden processes than was I, the communications I received generally focused on a principle of relationship or on a vision of what could unfold. Thus, while the questions initiating the communications presented in this chapter relate to specific events in the Findhorn garden, the communications themselves are basically philosophical. In some cases they describe ideals which may be beyond humanity's present capabilities of attunement but nevertheless provide a vision to inspire and ensoul its efforts.

It may be useful to describe briefly the processes I experience in receiving these communications. Put simply, it is a process of attuning to an inner, subjective state of mind which is in resonance with a larger more impersonal level of consciousness which I may wish to contact. Properly achieving this attunement is largely a matter of holding in the totality of my awareness (which includes thought and feeling and spiritual imagination) a sense of what I wish to contact and then relaxing into a sensitive, listening kind of attention. I find my identity blending with the identity of a particular *level* of consciousness and life, not necessarily with a particular *being.* However, resonating with that identification may be a life or a group mind representing a collective of lives, and I begin to participate in its identity and awareness. I remain myself, fully conscious as a human being, yet I become something else as well, in a deep empathetic relationship out of which information, meaning, insight and teaching can emerge.

Sometimes this emergence takes the form of words which I repeat, but usually it is a gestalt of images, feelings, insights and impressions which I must mentally translate into verbal form for the benefit of my listeners. Sometimes this is quite difficult, but usually the matrix of the contact itself acts like a guiding pattern on my mind and I find myself in a rhythm of speech and an awareness of special nuances of vocabulary and word order somewhat different from my normal conscious speech patterns. What I am communicating, therefore, is not just information but an experience. I am fully participating in the act of communion and communication, which, to my mind, makes it a substantially different process from the kind of passive channeling known in mediumship or in spiritualism.

For me, it is not a psychic experience but a mystical one, and the resulting communication is born out of the synergy and blending of several energies: my conscious mind, my higher conscious awareness of soul, the level with which I am communing, the being or beings representing that level and personifying its energies, the energies surrounding the people sharing the experience with me, and to some extent the energies of the environment which include the qualities of space/time, and the overall qualities and conditions of the moment within which the communication is occurring (i.e., is it the right place or the right time for certain information to be transmitted?). Thus, such a transmission represents the quality and characteristics of an act of communion beyond time and in time between the various forms of life involved, and to me the energy of that communion is always more important than the specific information or words that conveyed it.

The following communications, then, were born out of a particular need, but the act of communion to meet that need went beyond it and entered into deeper levels of concern regarding the role of man in nature and the question of dominance and synthesis. It is the meaning of these communications that is important as it relates to this question. Too often, attention is placed on phenomenal aspects—the contact itself, the nature spirits or the sensitives such as Roc, Dorothy or myself. While these phenomena may have importance on one level, it is the meaning arising from the acts of investigation and sharing, the meaning of these or other transmissions discussed in this book, that is ultimately important. I would, therefore, direct your earnest attention to the message itself and to the practical demonstration of that meaning and message within the Findhorn garden.

Transmission One: Cooperation with the Nature Spirits. The following communication is from a level and beingness that simply identifies itself as "John." Myrtle and I made contact with this presence at an early stage in our work. Since then, "John" has been a code name or contact point with a wide variety of energy lives whose true identities are rarely translatable into human personality terms. In this case, John identifies himself as an emissary, representing "the interests and the consciousness of the elemental kingdoms" involved in the Findhorn garden experiment. The occasion for this communication arose out of questions concerning the relationship of man's will, represented by Peter in the garden, and the will of the elementals or nature spirits.

John: *The elementals are not the physical body of a plant. A plant is a manifestation of the beingness of Earth, the ensouling life of the planet which you may call the Earth Logos. Plants serve a function for this being. They also serve the function of providing an environment for higher forms of life to enter and be comfortable within this physical dimension. The elementals, whom I represent, make possible the growth and development of natural forms.*

We are far more ancient for the most part than the physical Earth itself and we draw freely upon the powers of cosmic creativity. Before a planet can come into existence, we exist; we bring the planet into existence.

At one time, we were the sole masters of Earth. In a way, man developed from our womb, which you call nature. In part, man is a product of the elemental and devic kingdoms, for he was once a being like ourselves, attuned to creative, cosmic sources. When the form of man was created and humanity as you know it began to develop, we were his teachers. For ages, we guided and protected him. He responded to us because in his inmost sensitivity and remembrance, he was one with us. In the realm of our true beingness, we walked together as one.

However, there came a time when it was decided that to promote man's evolution and the accomplishment of his destiny, he was to be given the gift of creative thought, the gift of individuation and selfhood. This also implied the experience of separation, polarity and duality as part of the creative consciousness and power. Man

was set upon the road toward learning mastery in the use of that power. Within him and before him lay the power and the seed of authority to mold the Earth as he might see fit. He was given dominion over the Earth, in expectation that he would learn to use it wisely.

Our authority was never taken from us. However, we were told that man, to develop the potentials of his divinity and to prepare for a cosmic destiny, needed to be freed from that authority and from the possible domination of his being by the more powerful planetary forces of nature. To gain such freedom, he was placed in touch with the authority of his own being which he needed to understand in order to exercise wisdom, love and understanding in dealing with the needs of Earth and the rhythms of our work and life.

We, the elementals, the kingdom of builders and those who externalize form, do understand the needs of Earth. Because humanity shares the same source with us and is one with us on deep levels of being, mankind, too, has an inherent sensitivity to the needs of Earth and to the plan of God. But when man becomes overly lost in the development of his own self and obscures that inner knowledge, consequently acting insensitively and even hostilely towards his planet and its divinity, we have the right not to obey him. We cannot dispute man's authority. We simply withdraw and allow his creative power direct and unshielded access to the primeval forces of formation. Because man in such a state lacks the sensitivity, knowledge and wisdom with which we work these forces, he cannot control these basic energies. Being out of tune with his devic qualities, or what you would

call your soul consciousness, man attempts to express this creative authority through his mind alone, which is not broad enough, subtle enough or strong enough to fully encompass these energies. Hence, nature does not obey him as swiftly and perfectly as it does us.

We recognize that man has the right and obligation to create nature, to externalize the forms that reflect his own nature. However, when this right is stretched and man attempts to destroy the balance between us and to cloak all the planet in artificiality, there is conflict and difficulty. Man must learn that authority does not mean license. He himself, however evolved, is still part of the nature kingdom. Though he has dominion over nature, he cannot destroy it without destroying himself. The key to his expression of dominion is to first gain sovereignty of his own nature, then all other reflections of nature on a larger scale will willingly and joyously work with him.

If man continues to misunderstand the nature of his authority and dominion, he will destroy the ecological patterns of his planet and himself in the process. We cannot be destroyed, for we are beyond form. Neither can man's true nature be destroyed, although his form can. He can render his planet unfit for his form of life, thus cutting himself off from the chosen avenue of his unfoldment and evolution. This will have serious spiritual consequences for him. We will survive such an action; the evolving idea and image of man in his present form will not.

You have asked specifically about the role of man in nature and about the role of Findhorn and its garden.

Man's role is to tend the Earth as a steward. It is wrong for him to attempt to play the part of devic or elemental lord; that is our role. What man must do is exercise his creative, inspirational authority which is his true place in the scheme of things on Earth. Man is given the gift of creative imagination and must create the vision of what must be done. This power is equivalent to but in some ways exceeds that of the devas; it is man's God-power.

The elemental beings, under the authority of the being you call Pan, do not originate the patterns of Earth and of nature; we only build and

maintain them. We possess this great power because we are cosmic in our origins. It is man who has the authority and the potential to take the energies of life beyond these patterns and into new realms of possibilities and forms.

Gardening in the past has been man's attempt to externalize that potential and authority, but he has often approached this not in a spirit of unity and cooperation but in one of conquest, seeking to mold the Earth to his own pattern. This may be proper in essence but he has approached it insensitively and wrongly. He does not need to douse the earth with chemicals. He does not need to exercise brute force on the forms of nature to make them obey his designs. He must provide us free scope to work with him, in love, respect and cooperation.

But understand this: if we are limited solely to being servants of man, our power is curtailed. It is important that cooperation comes to mean something deeper than obedience, for in understanding us and cooperating with us, man will learn valuable lessons about himself, which is one of the objects of the exercise. Man's consciousness must expand to new insights and into deeper communion with and dominion over his own nature. Out of this can come a communion with us, a mating, if you will, that will embody a divine power to transform our planet.

To us, the experience of this center is an event of profound joy, for here we can participate in the kind of cooperation I am describing and witness the invocation of new and powerful energies. We see it as an outlet for us to reach into human consciousness and it gives us hope.

In working with you here, we must have an increasingly free hand; otherwise we cannot cope with the energies you are invoking, and we would have to withdraw. If you think you can yourself embody the nature energies to make this garden grow, then you are welcome to try, but how much greater it will be if we can work together. As the experiment of your garden continues, you must think of us and see us as perfect partners. Use your authority to encourage us, to have trust in us and to give us a greater freedom of action to pour our cosmic energies into this garden and into the

human beings who are part of it—for we seek union with the humans here, as well. Together we will produce a garden, a flowering, an abundance beyond anything human imagination can conceive of. This is our promise.

Man cannot grow unless he learns to understand his oneness with his world, with us. The necessary step for man is to draw out his nature heritage from his past being and elevate it. He will not become a deva or an elemental but something far greater, something that will release us and show us a new promise and a new path of growth. Our evolution and yours depends on it. That is why we cannot cater to your desires or simply be your servants, for then there is little incentive for you to really understand us and yourselves. If we see you manipulate and mutilate our plants, as you and most gardeners have been doing, in order to force them to meet your human-conceived requirements and images of perfection, ignoring their inherent divine perfection and doing nothing to help us encourage its unfoldment, then how can we blend with you? How can we achieve our joint destinies?

Question: Are you saying there must be changes made in the way the gardening is being done here at Findhorn?

John: *That is what I am saying. This is more than just a cooperative venture. We are not here to beautify this garden for the glory of any man but for the glory of God. We, too, are manifestations of God. Man is not our superior; we are not his superiors. We are lovers. We must become one if these new creative energies are to be utilized properly and not allowed to become destructive. We yearn for this oneness, but it must go beyond simple cooperation. Before anything is done in the garden, it must be considered from our point of view as well as from man's point of view.*

We are being directed by God to expose ourselves and become more vulnerable to man than we have ever permitted in the past since man lost his sense of communion with us, in order that you may approach us more directly and with greater ease within this center and others like it that may arise. If in the process of the experiment we are hurt through injurious actions to the forms we build and minister to, we will have patience and bear the hurt, knowing that you are learning. We do not mind if there is minor offense as you seek to learn a greater communion so long as you correct it and do not repeat it and are sensitive to our needs as they are revealed to you. We are aware of your motives and your intents. But if the hurts continue or the motives are less than sensitive to the whole, we must retreat under the law we obey. If we withdraw from this center due to your own lack of wisdom, it will lessen that healing force—the love, the peace, the hope, the light—that is flowing into the world from this and similar centers elsewhere where cooperation and attunement between our kingdoms is being explored and developed. Understand the responsibility you have taken on.

Transmission Two: The Dominion of Love. The following communication is one of several received in August, 1970, from an archetypal force calling itself "Limitless Love and Truth." (The story behind these transmissions and the text of them is contained in my book, *Revelation: The Birth of a New Age.* This particular communication was not included in that book as it specifically dealt with nature and with the Findhorn garden and seemed to be of a different theme than the other messages.)

Like the preceding message, this communication arose out of a need to understand the concept of man's dominion over the Earth. Findhorn was carrying out certain commonly accepted gardening practices, such as pinching side shoots off tomato plants in order to make the vitality of the plant go into the fruit rather than into the leaves. The same was being done to sweet peas in order to produce larger blossoms. Over a period of time, messages received from the elementals through Roc had said that this practice was, in effect, mutilation for man's purposes. During a session with Limitless Love and Truth, this question was brought up.

Limitless Love and Truth: *The key to your question lies in what I represent, limitless love. One who has been an inspiration of love to you, one who bore the embodiment of the Christ, said that he who would be the greatest of all must be the servant of all. In that statement lies full understanding. Man was never given dominion over the Earth to express it in a one-sided and isolated state of consciousness. Man's dominion arises from the fact that his soul is an interweaving of many patterns belonging to other kingdoms of evolution in a new synthesis of vision and expression. Man represents a more complex and potentially more advanced form, with a wider range of creative possibilities open to his consciousness, than other kingdoms of life within nature, although the devas and elementals express in their fashion a far more perfect attunement to their evolution and role than man as yet does to his.*

Man occupies a unique position because of his blended nature. A devic being can only see the world from the viewpoint of a deva, an elemental from the viewpoint of an elemental. A human being can potentially see it from both aspects and from others. This gives him a vaster creative scope.

This is his dominion: the power of love and the creative ability to express new vision. Man does not have to impose this vision upon nature. He must communicate it to nature and nature will respond, indeed, awaits to respond to man's true creative potential. If, on the other hand, man attempts to manipulate the physical forms of nature without a complementary understanding and communication with the inner side of nature, not only is he hindering communication, he is limiting his own powers.

The power of the nature kingdoms to effect complete transformation of physical form within a certain time period has already been placed before you. Man primarily needs only to communicate to the beings of nature what is required without any other physical activity on his part, save what attunement inspires him to provide as his participation in the process. This is a reflection of the equally great creative powers that humanity holds within itself, an ability to completely manipulate matter through the power of thought and spirit. You have many examples of human beings who have achieved a high level of attunement to God who manifest this ability. But this ability cannot be manifested safely nor purely nor properly in the New Age unless there is first a loving awareness and sense of caring and communion with all life forms, mineral, vegetable, animal and human, that may be influenced and affected by the use of this creative power.

Look upon your world. Man has done much to alter its face using physical methods. In some

cases he has created great good, but now he discovers that out of what appeared good, evil manifests as an imbalance in the life processes. Vast areas of land, water and air have been laid waste and poisoned and made highly negative within the etheric realms, posing danger to all life. It necessitates considerable effort on the part of the inner realms of life to protect physical life dimensions from these imbalanced energies. All this stems from what man has conceived as good actions from his limited point of view. He has chopped down the tree today for his own ends without realizing that he may be swept away tomorrow in the erosion of the soil.

Man must learn to commune with nature, for in order to properly exercise his creative dominion, he needs to have information, knowledge of the results of his actions, love, understanding and the ability to gain the cooperation of all who may be affected. The powers within man are potent. For his own safety and that of his world they cannot be fully actualized if they might be misused.

This new requirement of cooperating with the nature spirits that is being explored in this center

is not a loss to man of his dominion. It is a step of growth towards expressing that dominion differently, with more love and awareness, as God intended from the beginning. "He who would be the greatest of all must be the servant of all"—through love, through understanding, through cooperation. From this will come to man deep insights into his own being and potentials which will bring him freedom and greater creativity than he can now express. He who would embody and wield the will of God must be absolutely harmless, i.e., unable to harm another being through willfulness, ignorance or lack of love. This does not mean that love cannot destroy forms in order to give greater forms a chance to be born. But this power must be expressed through the law which embodies love, wisdom, awareness and attunement to the One.

God is within all life. The nature kingdoms are not less than you, nor greater; they are only different. They do not have the scope of action which you possess. Hence they look to you to lead them properly into greater realms of their own evolution by suggesting and conceiving for them newer and greater forms for their life energies to ensoul. Suggest new aspects of beauty and perfection, but understand that if this suggestion reflects only a human point of view, it will be difficult for the devic and elemental beings to fully comprehend what you wish. To gain their full cooperation and ability to work with you, you must be able to communicate, to some degree at least, on their terms and according to their values and vision.

The elemental and devic worlds are far more powerful than the human kingdom at the present time, for they are still within attunement to the energies of God. However, man holds within himself this vast creative sonship to God, but he must express it according to the pattern that God provides. God is not only the God of human beings. He is the Lord and the Lover, the Creator and the Nourisher, the Seed, the Promise and the Fulfillment of all forms of nature and of the Earth and of the cosmos beyond. To do God's will you must attempt to see with his vision, know with his love, live with his life. It is as simple as that. It is not a complex pattern.

As the session continued, the questions revolved around specific experiences within the garden. A question arose about dealing with the tomatoes and how to enlarge the fruit itself.

Limitless Love and Truth: *I understand that your concern is with food. Where does your food come from? God is your supply, not the vine nor the tree, nor the soil nor other humans, nor the kingdoms of nature. God is your source of supply. God is everywhere. He is not large. He is not small. A small fruit raised on a joyful plant filled with vitality holds more God-nourishment than a large fruit raised on a plant that has been mutilated and has therefore experienced pain and fear—negative*

energies which enter the fruit. It may provide more bulk in terms of quantity but there is less nourishment in terms of the God-energy within the fruit.

If you are anxious about your food, you do not trust God. It has been stated you shall have abundant food. If in your present condition you seek to raise food that is both large and plentiful but by using methods which suggest a lack of consideration for the viewpoint of the plant and its attendant nature beings—which, you understand, must see things from their perspective just as you do from yours—that plant cannot help but respond with pain, fear and anger, because it doesn't understand what is happening to it. Even if it should understand, it will still respond with pain to actions that mutilate it. Such actions born of anxiousness and inconsiderateness weaken your powers of manifestation, which are rooted in your attunement to the Whole.

I have stated that the power and laws of manifestation can only function best where there is love. This should be understandable to you, for otherwise the laws of manifestation degenerate into the essence, if not the forms, of black magic. Love and communion, on the other hand, help you to manifest things in harmony with all who are involved. If the kingdoms of nature see that your love is greater than your anxiety for food, then, in honor of the God we all serve, they will pour their cooperative energies into the manifestation of all that you may need, not always in terms of size or amount but always in the greater values of quality, the quality of life that, coming from God, is the ultimate nourishment.

Man, in his isolated consciousness, seeking dominion over the Earth, has violated and exploited nature. As is suggested by these communications from nature, and by others received at Findhorn over the years, there are beings of the invisible kingdoms of nature that regard humanity as a nuisance at best, a dangerous disruptive source of negativity at worst. That they are counterbalanced by others who do recognize the role and value of man is no consolation.

There is a subtle and important difference between humanity and the kingdoms of nature. Though biologically and psychically nature has been his womb and mother, spiritually, man harkens from a different source. His identity is not to be found in nature alone, but within himself in relationship to that Source. It is one of the traditions of the esoteric wisdoms that humanity needed to be separated from the powerful forces of instinctive, unconscious energies of nature and that the mechanism used to this end was the promotion of the experience of selfhood. Domination of nature by man has proved unhealthy, but so is the domination of man by nature.

The solution definitely lies in understanding the meaning of dominion. Is it rule by force and tyranny, or is it leadership through love, example, communion, understanding, caring? In Genesis, God is not giving dominion to another of Earth's creatures; he is affirming the dominion of a being made in his image. An image is more than a form; it is the life-process from which forms expressing its various stages arise. The image of God is the process of divinity itself, and that is a process of growth, of nourishment, of wisdom, light and love. It is the process of life unfolding itself into greater levels of freedom and knowing and expression.

The capability of embodying this process with self-consciousness and awareness distinguishes humanity from all other kingdoms. Man has the divine power of transcendence, of moving beyond pre-set patterns, of bridging the dimensions of form and spirit, potential and actuality, image and fulfillment. Humanity is the Race of the Garden, the Race of Eden, expelled from paradise in order to discover how to be paradise's creator and not just its child. Man is learning how to be a gardener on all levels, a co-creator with God, a re-creator of the Earth.

Towards this destiny all the kingdoms of nature look and work with hope, hope in the ability of mankind to employ selfhood with wisdom and love and thus create freedom for all. It is no wonder that a place like Findhorn is watched with such attention, for it is an experiment in reaching for that destiny. It is a garden where men may learn the true nature of their dominion, born not out of their beingness as men but out of their beingness as gods. This is a dominion based on participation in the wholeness of life and not on the strength of one of life's aspects over the others.

At Findhorn, man retains his ancient role of dominance but it is through communion, communication and the arts of community. Through his dominance, none are made low but all are exalted. The kingdoms of nature are not seen as forms to be manipulated or as lesser beings of evolution but as the brothers and lovers which they have always sought to be. Findhorn does not seek to return to primitive forms of nature worship or the surrender of man's consciousness to the instinctive drives of the wild, elemental energies. Rather it demonstrates the calling forth and the transforming of those energies through the consciousness of self-aware and attuned individuals, secure in their oneness with God and therefore active in their oneness with the Earth. Out of separation comes synthesis, and out of domination comes cooperation. This is the promise of recreating the Garden that is Earth's essence.

In the words of Limitless Love and Truth: *God is not only the God of human beings. He is the Lord and the Lover, the Creator and the Nourisher, the Seed, the Promise and the Fulfillment of all the forms of nature and of the Earth. . . .* As we are his image made flesh, we can strive to be no less. It is not a complex pattern. We see ourselves reflected in our actions. If we would discover the promise of the divine image within us, our actions must reflect the wholeness and love of the Nourisher and the Promise, the Seed and the Fulfillment, moving us towards the One. From dominance to synthesis and beyond. . . . It is as simple as that.

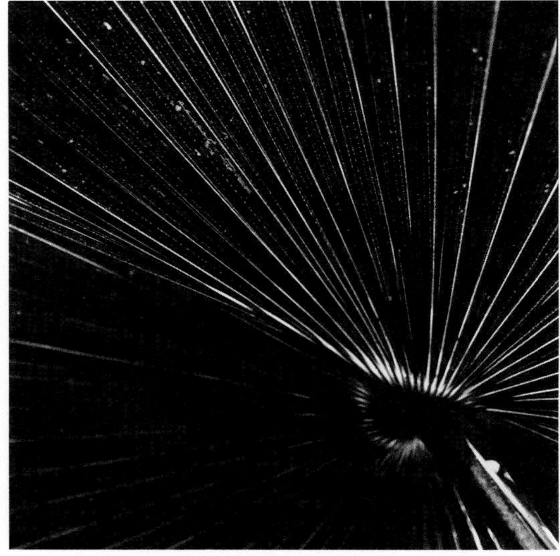

ROSEMARY

You do not suddenly jump into consciousness of all this. It is gradually that you become aware of My life all around you.

THE GARDEN TODAY

THE SEQUEL. A visitor to the Findhorn garden today would find it quite different from the phenomenal young garden Peter created in the mid-'60s. Cabbages are back to their average weight of three to four pounds each, and foxgloves once more aspire to reach four rather than eight feet. In many places the sandy base of the soil is barely visible beneath layers of compost. The laburnum, eucalyptus and pine saplings that Peter brought in now tower above the hypericum, spiraea and wild rose bushes, interspersed with hundreds of varieties of flowers and ground cover. It is a beautiful garden, growing in a rather unlikely place. But is this all that makes the Findhorn garden unique enough to call special attention to it?

Certainly, in the earlier years, it was distinguished from other gardens by the fact that its gardeners were advised by God's voice through Eileen, the devas speaking through Dorothy, the nature spirits through Roc, and other levels of reality contacted by David. But this situation could not continue indefinitely. In 1973 Dorothy and David returned to the United States with a group of several others to form the Lorian Association in California. In late 1974 the inner voice that had been speaking to Eileen for more than twenty years took on a new and less separative aspect. The form of recorded messages that was necessary during the creation of Findhorn's foundations gave way to Eileen's growing recognition that God is truly within every moment and every individual, not separate but infinitely varied. In spring of 1975, Roc passed out of his physical body into a realm of existence where he may now be more at one with his beloved nature spirits. Peter's powerful initiating energies are increasingly focused on the expanding community and Findhorn's public role. It might appear that the garden has become just another aspect of community life. Does this mean that the experiment in cooperation between man and nature is over? Without the assistance of those sensitives who can tune into the nature forces directly, is man once again left alone in the garden?

If so, the Findhorn garden as created by Peter in cooperation with the devas and nature spirits would be nothing more than history, a remarkable event in time. Does it have anything now to offer the rest of us, seeking a way to make ourselves and our planet whole? The answer is found in both the subsequent history of the garden and the beauty that it reveals today.

In 1970 when Peter turned his focus toward other areas of the community, the next phase of the garden experiment began. But it was certainly not in terms anyone was expecting. A series of professional and non-professional gardeners with varying levels of attunement to the devas and nature spirits passed through the garden during the following years. The needs of the expanded community kept any of them from devoting their total time and energy to it, as Peter had. The community was now committed to the growth of human consciousness through various work and study programs.

In spring of 1974 the new University Hall, being designed and built by community members to serve as a center of creative expression, became the focus of attention. In the excitement over the flowering of human consciousness it seems we were overlooking its seed-bed. The garden was in danger of imperceptibly passing out of our awareness.

That same spring, most of the group who had been involved in the garden for the previous three years either moved into other work patterns or left the community. Others with a great deal of love for nature but with little technical background in horticulture became the gardeners. "We just plugged away the best we could, the best we knew how for the garden." Meanwhile, the glow of the plants began to fade.

Then Fred Barton arrived in the community, with forty years experience as an amateur and professional gardener and an encyclopedic memory for the Latin names and the origins of every tree, shrub and flower that grows in Britain, and their care. His wisdom was derived from years of study and fond observation of nature—but Fred didn't hear, see or feel what were called nature spirits or devas. He was aware only of the power and wonder in nature that he experienced through working with plants. "When I knew I was going to move to Findhorn, I kept wondering how I would ever be able to marry up what I felt and knew about gardening in a practical way with the method of consciousness that seemed to be taught here. In the back of my mind, I was convinced that they had to be the same thing." Were all of Fred's years of study worthless when these Findhorn people were saying they could respond to a plant's needs simply by tuning into the devas or by merely beaming love at it? By the looks of the garden, it was obvious to everyone that this was not so. But whenever Fred said, with care and concern in his heart for the plants, "Prune that *fagus sylvatica purpurea,*" or "Cut back that arabis, it's strangling the crocuses," three-quarters of the gardeners, with care and concern in *their* hearts for the plants, would protest, "No, that hurts them, and we've been asking the devas to do something about it instead," or "Maybe they like being close together like that."

By the time the semi-annual visitors' conference was held in autumn of 1974, the garden group was stymied by what seemed to be two irreconcilable approaches to gardening. The topic of this conference was "Man, Nature and the New Age"—and the focus was on the garden. Dorothy and Roc arrived on the scene, and the age-old tensions between man and nature erupted. At times it seemed that the conference was contributing more to raising questions than to raising consciousness. "What does cooperation with devas and nature spirits mean in practical terms for *my* garden?" "What is the difference between cooperation and manipulation?" "What is gardening anyway?" Nature and man still had different answers it seemed. Where would the experiment go from here?

The conference did serve to refocus some of the community's attention back onto the garden, but the gardeners themselves remained in conflict. Fred was a gardener and didn't need tutoring on the growth of consciousness to know how to grow a successful garden. Nor did he have the kind of spiritual background that Peter had had which would allow him to readily accept the reality of devas and nature spirits. Most of the gardeners, on the other hand, were convinced that the knowledge of the devas was essential to gardening, and they were opposed to the manipulation of nature expressed in certain traditional horticultural practices. The gardening group almost left Fred; Fred almost left the gardening group—and the garden just patiently waited. But clarity was inevitable once the poles got far enough apart. At a certain point, all of the gardeners began to realize that their main concern was not which technique they were going to use, but rather why they were all working in the garden. Their common meeting ground was their love for nature's creation, and that made them want to work with her in their own small way through gardening. Through love and open minds, communication and blending began. As man cooperated with man, sharing knowledge and perceptions, man began to cooperate with nature in a new way.

The experiment was evolving. In its initial stages, Peter, Eileen, Dorothy and Roc had each represented separate and unique aspects of the energies needed to create the garden at Findhorn in cooperation with God and nature. This separation made clear the positions and contributions of each aspect. And even the sand gave rise to abundant life. But once this sand was converted into viable soil and traditional gardening techniques were known and applied, what was the next step in cooperation?

The founders of Findhorn were not establishing a set pattern that had to be imitated in order to cooperate with nature. To recreate your bit of earth, you don't need a dynamo like Peter, a channel for God's voice like Eileen, a free spirit like Dorothy to receive advice from the devas, and a wizard like Roc to talk with elementals and nature spirits. To place the emphasis on the form of the experiment rather than the essential message would be to miss the point. God, the devas and the nature spirits are all aspects of one life, the same life we are expressing. They are, in fact, within us, and each of us has the power to work with these forces to create Heaven on Earth. Recognizing this and acting upon it was the challenge the gardeners were facing in 1974—the challenge of a change of consciousness.

In the unity of life, spirit and matter are both divine. Each gardener, then, is responsible for nurturing the spirit and the form of the plants in his garden by finding the knowledge of the devas deep within and blending this in action with practical gardening techniques. In time Fred was not only reading but studying deva messages. "I have found here a far greater consciousness in regard to plants and gardening than I have ever had before. I wouldn't have believed it possible, because I have always had a deep caring for plants. But this knowledge of the devas and nature spirits has lifted gardening for me beyond a process like turning nuts and bolts on a machine and given it a new vitality. Yet the job itself remains anchored in the earth and pulls down what I feel to be a divine power, so that in working with plants, one really feels them to be a living part of oneself. Before this, my feelings about plants were more nebulous, and I couldn't convey what I experienced working with them to anybody else, other than perhaps saying that the power I felt is what gave people 'green thumbs.' I find that now I have a new set of tools to use to convey my feelings and to listen to the feelings of others. And so our misunderstandings are overcome." The other gardeners, too, were learning a new set of tools. Listening to Fred and asking questions, they were absorbing the knowledge and wisdom man has gained since first inviting plants to live with him rather than just around him. In Fred's terms, "We are mixing it all together and in the end we shall have what you might call a beautiful compost."

Soon the structure of the University Hall was growing side by side with a garden once more radiant and vital. Both were rising out of the awareness that all forms of life seek to express the fullness of their identity. The unfolding of human consciousness cannot be separated from the unfolding of the total environment in which it finds expression. Both must grow, or neither can grow. As the gardeners recognize the divinity inherent in all aspects of the plants they are caring for, all reveal their true essence. Thus, the real beauty of the Findhorn garden, and of any garden, lies in the radiance of its plants and its gardeners, both turning toward the light.

Peter, as representative of man creating the garden, was surrounded by individuals to whom God and the angels were as real as they were to Adam and Eve in the Garden of Paradise. While Peter, in innocence, was able to accept this reality, it yet remained external to him. The experience of the garden and the gardeners in 1974 was to find this reality within. Adam and Eve had to fall from the state of unconscious innocence into the world of apparent opposites in order to learn that the dialogue of the opposites speaks of oneness. They themselves were not separate from each other or from the world around them, but through each other and through the wilderness in which they found themselves, they could once again create that garden of harmony that God creates. Now we, their children, can join hands with nature and re-enter Eden, no longer barred by the angel with the burning sword but in the company of the angelic hierarchy, the devas and the nature spirits.

In this chapter the Findhorn gardeners share what it is like to work in the garden today, putting into action the wisdom and insights of the devas and nature spirits. However, the essence of the garden lies not only in the specific information that is included here but also in the shared experience of joy and commitment that is felt by the gardeners in their work. The questions and answers have been drawn from discussions that took place during the conference on Man, Nature and the New Age as well as from questions the gardeners often ask themselves. Hopefully, these will be helpful guidelines for those who wish to explore cooperation with nature in their own way, for the return to the Garden is not only happening in the Findhorn garden today. It is happening in *your* garden today.

QUESTIONS AND ANSWERS

Would you tell me something about the Findhorn garden today and your daily work pattern?

About six of us tend the garden as our main work program. While we range in age from seventeen to near seventy, it is a basic love for the earth and all her creatures that has drawn us together here to cultivate both ourselves and this garden. Depending upon the season and the daily needs of other work programs, we are joined by a varying number of others who choose to work part-time in the garden, as well as guests visiting the community.

We start each work day with an "attunement." Joining hands, we stand together in a circle in silence. During this minute or two, each gardener consciously blesses the day, his or her fellow gardeners, the nature kingdoms and the day's work before us. We become aware of our individual energies blending with the energies of everyone and everything in our environment at that moment. Following the attunement, we discuss the work

design for the day, taking into account the weather and various on-going garden projects. Our group coordinators, or "focalizers" as we call them, keep the garden's needs and our energies in focus, and they guide us in revealing the best overall plan of work for the day. Then, gathering our tools, we set out in various groups to collect seaweed, turn compost or work in any of the several garden areas that are part of the three acres upon which the community now lives.

"Flexibility in all things" has become a favorite Findhorn motto, and the weather is its most faithful teacher. Within one day at Findhorn, a gardener can catch a faceful of rain, sleet or snow, and then, most gratefully, a blast of sunshine.

Below the spacious sky that brings us this array of weather lies the three-mile-long Findhorn peninsula, a product of millennia of receding seas and scouring winds. While some areas of the land are suitable for farming, the larger part consists of sand dunes covered with a rugged growth of couch grass, heather, broom and gorse. The Findhorn community is located about midway down this peninsula. We are bordered on the east by a one hundred acre farm. In summer, the ripening barley crop there dances like waves on the sea; in winter, the land is still, sandy and bare. Just a quarter mile to the south of us is the Kinloss Royal Air Force Base where thundering transport jets and jaguar fighters can be heard and seen lifting off or touching down any time of day or night. On the north we are bordered by several acres of young evergreens that have been planted by a neighbor who is a conservationist. A mile beyond these trees, over sand dunes and through thickets of gorse, lies the North Sea. On still nights, the pounding of the surf on the pebbles of the beach sounds but a stone's throw from the community. Findhorn Bay defines our western boundary. There the brown peat-filled waters of the Findhorn River meet with the salty tides of the Moray Firth. Findhorn Village, a lively summer center for North Sea yachting, is located at the mouth of the Bay, on the tip of the peninsula.

In our garden in the Findhorn Bay Caravan Park, the fine calciferous sea sand of this peninsula has been transformed through the cooperation of man and nature over a period of more than ten years. The light but productive soil of the central garden area supports the shrubs, trees and formal flower beds which surround the caravans, bungalows and community buildings. Near the

Community Center, which houses the kitchen and dining room, is the original garden created by Peter which still supplies us with vegetables such as lettuce, radishes, parsley and marrow in the summer and hardy vegetables such as savoy cabbage, kale and leeks in late winter. Despite the fact that we are further north than Moscow, the Gulf Stream flowing past the British Isles keeps the temperature reasonably mild all year. Thus, an average growing season can extend from March through October, though we can sometimes have frosts into June and as early as September.

Adjacent to the Community Center, tucked into a thirty by sixty foot area between two caravans is our herb garden. Designed by Dawn MacLeod, a specialist in Britain on the planting and use of herbs, this garden is a beautiful pattern of shapes,

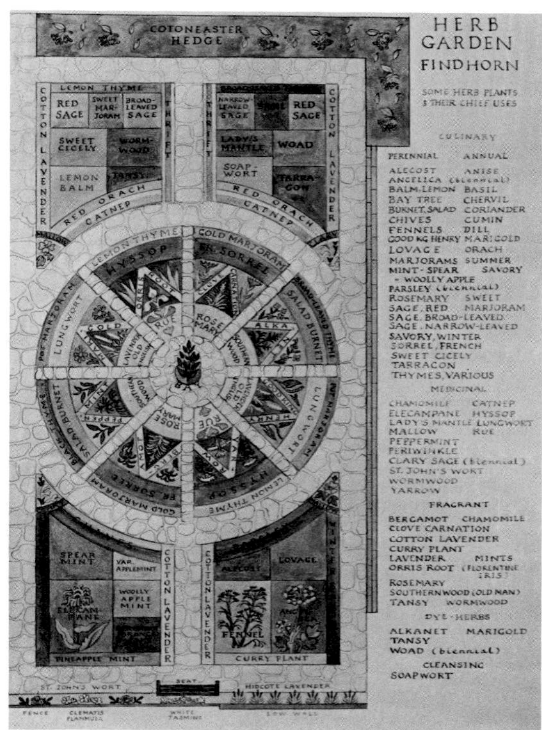

colors and fragrances. The fresh herbs that supply us with teas, seasonings and herbal remedies throughout the summer are dried in autumn for our winter use. A bench has been placed in this garden, for we have found that just being in the presence of these plants has a soothing effect.

A narrow tarmac road leads from the center of the community, past our two greenhouses, the nursery beds and the wild garden, toward the area called Pineridge. There the craft studios are located, as well as more caravans and bungalows. Besides the small gardens surrounding these homes, a "controlled natural garden" has been designed and planted in what was formerly an open field of gorse, broom and heather. At one time the park owner had cleared this land for proposed caravan sites. When the local planning board refused permission, he brought in several truckloads of brown, sandy loam to hold down the exposed and shifting sands. The natural seed hidden in this new soil exploded into more than fifty species of wild flowers—among them hawkweed, harebell, crane's-bill and wild chamomile. Now, with the

permission of the park owner, a natural garden has been created, where wild flowers grow among trees and shrubs recently planted by us. In a few years, a young wood of silver birch, sycamore and pine will rise above broom, senecio and cotoneaster shrubs. As Fred, the initiator and designer of this garden has said, "It is primarily for the sake of the tiny wild flowers that we are creating this controlled natural garden. These wild plants will establish themselves amidst the hardy shrubs we plant. It's up to us to work with nature here, observe her wild state, feel her presence and recreate this garden in imitation of her. Control on our part is merely in creating paths so we can view the wonder of her work, and placing benches where we can sit quietly to listen to the birds that will be attracted here. Some mistakes, like planting shrubs too close together, might happen and, of course, we will have to remedy this situation, but if nature sees that we are willing to cooperate, she will readily accept our mistakes. The gorse, heather and grasses that grew quite naturally here were at one time removed, yet we saw nature spring back with a glorious abundance of wild seed. I often marvel at the way in which nature, battered by man, springs back time and time again. The devas and nature spirits never forget the earth, it is only man who forgets."

Besides these gardens located within the community environs, six miles to the southwest of us is a third of an acre of land which is also a community garden. Easily four times larger than our local vegetable garden, this plot promises us new ventures in cooperation. Through observation and experience there, our understanding of companion

planting, weed and animal control and experimentation with varied vegetable strains is being deepened. Several afternoons a week, an open invitation is extended to the community to join us in working with this land.

A vital part of our day's work is the mid-morning break together. During this half hour in our potting shed over tea and coffee, buttered bread and biscuits, we might experience an atmosphere filled with the silence and peace of the devas or the tumbling laughter of the nature spirits. It is a time to become better acquainted with each other and the guests who have joined us, to reflect on our morning's experiences, to share new awarenesses or discuss some practical course of action in the garden. Our work as gardeners is underlined by the same principles of education that are at work in all areas of life at Findhorn, drawing out of us further expressions of the one life inherent in all life.

Since classes, other work programs and meetings are often scheduled in the afternoons, the work pattern for the rest of the day is not as tightly organized. It is then up to each gardener to be aware of areas of individual responsibility in the garden and to balance this out with these other activities.

We realize that it is not just the practical work of the gardeners that keeps the plants vital and glowing. The Findhorn garden belongs to everyone, and essential to its life is the consciousness and love given by each community member, each guest and visitor, and the energy of the devas and nature spirits with whom we work. When we give our love to these plants, the response that comes back to us is a warm and tangible experience. They communicate with us on whatever level we choose to approach them.

Do you see or talk to devas and nature spirits?

Everyone feels and experiences contact with the devas or nature spirits in his or her own way. Those individuals whose contact with these realms takes a form as definite as Roc's ability to see nature spirits or Dorothy's way of communicating with the devas are the exception. There is presently no one at Findhorn who is in contact in that way. In its simplest form, loving a plant or the rain or the sun is a link with the devas and nature spirits. Merely acknowledging their existence is communication with them, although their response may not be verbal or visual. The devas and nature

spirits are aware of such acknowledgment and respond with their love as we give them ours.

Fred: Sometimes in the silence of a wood I have heard something—an unusual sound, and then there's a movement. A bird . . . or was it a bird? Or I have heard a brook running—the water tinkles, suddenly the note changes. Was that the brook or was it something else? I can't tell. And again suddenly there is a whistling—is it the wind? No, there was no wind. But never have I seen anything.

Holger: Working in the garden, I've never actually hoped or asked that the nature spirits reveal themselves to me in the form of gnomes or elves. I'm just aware that they're there, and I don't want to limit them or myself by saying, "Well, I'm not sure you're there—show yourself." I don't even want to limit them by verbal communication, so although I do talk with them, it's more like an attunement than a conversation. What I really want to do is to consciously work with them to help bring back the balance man has upset on Earth.

Sono: I cannot with my present consciousness perceive God directly, nor can I perceive the nature spirits. But coming here and working in the garden, I have learned that they do exist. Now, it is as if the sun is just behind a cloud; I know the sun is there, even though I cannot see it at this time. That is how I feel about the devas and nature spirits. I know they are there, and just knowing that has made me feel closer to the divine in all things.

Michael: Last week when I was walking alone in the woods, I decided to concentrate on every sound. I sat down, looking at some flies and listening. One

of them landed on a pine needle as I watched. But I thought I also *heard* it land on the pine needle. It was incredible, that sound. To me, this is a bridge between our different perspectives in viewing nature spirits. I had decided not to look for anything outside of what was purely there on the physical plane—just what I could hear and see with my ears and eyes. And I found that it is just exactly through what you are doing, looking at the "real" things, that suddenly another realm opens. It is not by *wanting* to experience another realm that you get there, but by being completely aware of every action, every sound and color around you.

What is cooperation with nature besides tuning into and communicating with devas and nature spirits?

It would be a mistake to see cooperation with nature only as talking to devas and nature spirits. Letting humans know that they exist is certainly not the only reason why the devic realms have made themselves known to us. They wish to share with us what they already know—that behind the outer forms we are all brothers and sisters in the divinity we share. You don't have to be growing a garden to be cooperating. You can be driving down a highway and bless and acknowledge the life in the trees you are passing and your oneness with them, and you will be cooperating.

Contact with the devic realms is an education in the experience of wholeness. They have taught us to be aware of everything with which we share life on this planet, not only plants but also minerals and the machinery we make from them, animals and our fellow humans. We must come to view these other inhabitants of Earth as innately divine and recognize that they deserve our acceptance and respect.

Machines, too, respond to human love and care. All of you have had experiences of this but have not usually registered the implications because they seemed nonsensical to the mind. We would not belittle the mind, for through it we were brought to birth. But behind the mind, empowering it, are forces of even greater strength which we would ask you to use when you deal with machines. Metals are part of the one life; treat them as such and you will get a response. Bring joy to the world of metal by cooperating with us.

Machine Deva

What sort of rules are followed in the garden at Findhorn?

We don't have any gardening rules as such, for rules would limit something that is growing and evolving each day. While basically we follow organic gardening practices and procedures, we are working to develop conscious communication with the plants and the divinity inherent in them. This has made us constantly examine our motives and change many of our gardening practices.

Always warning plants before doing anything to them—pulling weeds, transplanting, pruning, cutting the grass—might be considered a rule we

follow, but essentially this just means loving the plants and therefore letting them be aware of and share in our actions. Once we have warned a plant about an impending change, we give it time to accept that change and be ready for it. While it might take one tree only a few hours to adjust to the prospect of being transplanted, it might take a few weeks for another. Here again, we can't make a rule because it is a matter of developing an intuitive sense of when a plant is ready for a change. It is far more important to open the lines of communication than to establish rules. Communication, however, is not necessarily talking to plants with words but rather coming into that unity with them that makes us aware of their needs and how best to help them grow. As Roc has said, "Love is always the fundamental key in guiding our awareness of a plant's needs."

Dorothy: One of the reasons for growing a garden is to develop an attunement with nature, with all life. It is up to each one of us as individuals with free will to make our own contacts with plants and establish cooperation with them. We are not here to give or to be given rules; we are here to find this attunement.

What is the attitude in the Findhorn garden toward weeds?

Strong negative connotations have developed around the term "weed," which simply refers to a wild flower growing where man does not want it. Living in their native environment, these wild flowers naturally grow more vigorously than non-indigenous plants we might invite into our garden. We are trying to see beyond the negative label weeds have been given by consciously acknowledging and appreciating all plants as divine creations, while yet remaining aware of our responsibility to create conditions that encourage the cultivated plants in our garden.

Nature, left to herself, remains in balance. So we are trying to watch nature and learn from her. We have noticed in our garden that particularly virile weeds do not seem to grow as readily around plants that are vibrantly healthy. It is up to us to insure health for the plants through both our thoughts and satisfying their physical needs. The devas told Dorothy that weeds have a part to play and that they come up where they are needed. It may be that particular wild flowers have qualities that can supply something the soil needs. Or it may be that nature tries in this way to indicate an imbalance that man has brought about in creating strains of flowers and vegetables that look good but do not have the strength and vibrancy of those which she would create on her own. We are aware of the research that has been done on the symbiotic relationship existing between various kinds of plants, and we feel there is also much we can learn in this area.

In a garden where one is trying exclusively to grow cultivated vegetables and flowers, it is up to the gardener to decide what the balance between natural and cultivated growth is to be. When weeds do begin to encroach on other plants and must be removed, they should be warned and pulled up with an attitude of love. As we pull them, we ask the deva of these wild flowers to transfer the energies to the plants of the same kind in our wild garden or our natural garden where nature remains undisturbed. We then put the weeds in the compost where they can give of themselves in an active way to the garden as a whole.

The problem of weeds brings us very much to the heart of what cooperation is because for many people gardening is predominantly a war—against weeds, weather, insects and the like. As Roc has suggested, "Perhaps man projecting aggression and hatred towards weeds makes them aggressive in return. Maybe if we love them, they will not have the need to be aggressive." As attitudes change, gardening practices also change from conflict with nature to cooperation and love.

How do you get rid of insects?

First of all, we try to see that our desire to get rid of them is out of consideration for the plant as well as the fact that we want the food the insects are eating. As far as the insects themselves are concerned, we recognize that they too have a part to play in the one life and should be approached with an attitude of love to reach a solution that is for the highest good of all concerned. It is normal for plants to live with a balanced population of insects around them. We have observed that healthy plants are not harmed by the insects they attract, just as healthy bodies are not infected by the germs they come in contact with.

However, imbalances in the insect population do occur in our garden. Through Dorothy and Roc, we have found out that this often is an indication that we are doing something not in keeping with the level of cooperation we have committed ourselves to. So, as well as dealing with the insects themselves, we must also consider what it might be in the garden that has brought about the imbalance. Perhaps the plants are not receiving what they need for their development. However, the source of the imbalance may be something that on the surface seems to be totally unrelated, such as the use of certain gardening practices that are offensive. It may also be due to the general upset in the balance of nature that man has brought about by the use of substances that are harmful to some other form of life, such as insecticides which poison birds. One part of nature cannot be isolated from another, so action taken against any part sets up a chain of events that affects the whole.

One method of dealing with insects is to contact the group soul or the deva of the insect concerned.

Acknowledging that it has a place in the scheme of things, you can explain your point of view, telling them that they are harming plants you want for your nourishment. It is important to suggest a specific place for them to go to when they leave. Since you wouldn't want to send them to your next door neighbor, this points out the ultimate need for a broader perspective in viewing the balance of nature on the whole planet rather than just seeking an immediate solution to the problem.

If the insects do not leave, it may be that either you have not been clear or committed enough in your communication with the group soul or that perhaps you have not tried to remedy the situation that brought about the imbalance in the first place. When we have found no other immediate solution and it is not possible to let them remain, we have either removed the insects by hand or used an organic spray of our own making. In either case they have been warned beforehand and we have disposed of them with an attitude of love and recognition, accepting full responsibility for what we are doing.

Do you prune plants?

We are aware that pruning is painful to plants, so we try to do only what is absolutely necessary and helpful, with plenty of advance warning. It is not just our desires to have clear pathways and beautiful hedges that must be taken into account in pruning, but as the consciousness of the elemental kingdoms has expressed through David, *Before anything is done in the garden, it must be considered from our point of view as well as from man's point of view.* Pruning is necessary and helpful, for example, when two plants are encroaching on one another. However, the gardener is responsible for knowing, for instance, how large shrubs are going to grow when he plants them so that they are placed far enough apart to minimize the need for pruning.

Another pruning practice we still engage in at Findhorn is with hybrid tea roses. Since they have been bred for generations to be cut back to encourage new growth and blooms, we felt it would be unfair to suddenly discontinue the practice. It would be comparable to opening the cage door to free a pet canary, expecting it to survive in the wild. At this point, we do not honestly know whether the extensive cutting back that is needed with this strain of roses arises from manipulation or from cooperation with nature. There are as many opinions among us as there are gardeners. We are aware of being in an interim period when it is necessary to build a bridge between the old and the new. We have been told by Roc that eventually we can ask the nature spirits to adjust the form of the plant on the etheric and they will do so, thus eliminating the need for extensive pruning. We gardeners as a group have a strong preference for shrub roses and hope that one of the future

experiments in cooperation will be the development of cultured roses that will not need pruning. It seems, in this case, that man's conception of beauty might need to be looked at.

Pruning, however, does seem to have its place in the scheme of things. In the wilderness, many shrubs, trees and plants are "pruned" naturally by the wind or by animals who use them for food. When they are taken from their natural environment and placed in a cultivated garden, the gardener must remain sensitive to their natural rhythm.

Roc: It is entirely up to man whether to continue his dominion or to cooperate, and it is up to man at what speed this cooperation develops. Certain practices, such as pruning, are still done and are accepted, but it is the attitude with which they are done that matters most. One should always bear in mind that as these gardening practices continue, ultimate cooperation is pushed a little further ahead into the future.

How do you make compost at Findhorn?

As with all aspects of life at Findhorn, our method of making compost is derived from many sources of knowledge—friends, books and contact with the devic realms, among them. Without relying solely on any one technique, a unique form has arisen that is appropriate for our resources and circumstances. Therefore, rather than passing on all the specific

steps we follow in creating compost, we would like to share with you our general method as well as the consciousness with which we experience the process.

Basically, composting is making soil. So we look at the way nature creates humus and adapt the process. This is not just a matter of throwing together a lot of ingredients and expecting them to explode into a living substance. As in all alchemical processes, balance, precision and timing are necessary.

By general observation of the area that surrounds Findhorn, we have come across the materials we use in our compost. The sea yields a variety of seaweeds. From our own garden, we use weeds, grass

cuttings, annuals we pull out in the autumn, and the green vegetable waste from our kitchen. We get chicken manure from the same dairy that supplies our milk and eggs. The neighboring farmer and the riding stables down the road have given us straw and their pig and horse manure—sometimes this is in exchange for labor. We collect leaf mold from the beech wood on nearby Cluny Hill. We have found that it is important to watch the balance the trees themselves are creating in their environment, and not deprive them for the sake of our needs. So, first we attune to a tree and ask whether or not it needs all the leaf mold beneath it for its own cycle. A strip of land bordering a pine forest five or six miles from here supplies us with wild grass cuttings. Here, too, is the huge pile of wood chips Peter drew upon to create his first compost heaps. These chips of pine tree bark were left over from some clearing done by the forestry service many years ago, and they are still contributing to our compost.

We prefer to mix the materials together in building each heap rather than layering them. We feel this gives a richer and more unified compost. The average life cycle of each bin is about three months, and we use most of this compost as soon as it is ready. Complete spreadings are given to the garden twice a year, spring and autumn.

Compost is not just a physical substance but a medium through which we can give love to the garden. By working to create compost we show our willingness to contribute our time and energy to the life of the plants. It is a cooperative effort of the gardeners, our co-workers such as earth worms and bacteria, the ingredients themselves, the elementals and the energy of the devas. Through making compost we are participating together in the essential process of creation.

Holger: Each compost heap is totally unique, not only because of the physical ingredients put into it but also the love and the consciousness of the different people who have been working on it. We are actually building the body of a living being. If

you tune into the being you are creating and to the elementals who are helping you work with the compost, they can tell you the particular needs of a heap. So often we've been working on a heap and someone has said something like, "I don't know why, but we've got to add more leaf mold to this mix." Even if that's completely different from the last mix, we go ahead, knowing it's the right thing to do. This is really a combination of practical know-how and attunement. If you attune to the area you live in, you find the materials you need for a good compost; if you attune to your compost heap, you know what the proper mixture and timing are for it.

Tom: What we really have to learn is how to treat the soil as a living entity. The soil is alive but a lot of agricultural practices seem to have been directed at just reaping its benefit by putting on fertilizers and taking out crops—without respect for the soil itself. If we understand that we are cooperating with the soil as part of a creative process, then we will help to establish a balance in nature.

Holger: In working on the compost heaps, I have found that a simple object like a pitchfork has an identity and its own characteristic energy. I find that if I hang onto a pitchfork tightly and make it do what I want, by the end of the day I am exhausted. But if I hold the fork loosely, just balancing it and not imposing my will on its will, it becomes an extension of myself and we flow easily, without resistance. If we recognize the living entity of that pitchfork, we can learn how to use it properly.

If I cooperate with the devas and nature spirits in my garden, will it be obviously different from a garden grown any other way?

Cooperation does not mean, for instance, that you will automatically grow huge plants in your garden as happened at Findhorn during the early years. You might, but that is not the aim or the essence of cooperation. When conscious contact with nature began at Findhorn, even the devas did not know what would happen in the garden. For all concerned, it was an experiment, an adventure in man coming to know and share in the oneness of life and the divine harmony that surrounds him all the time.

The essential point to keep in mind is that your garden reflects you. So the difference cooperation will make there will depend upon the change in your consciousness as it expands to recognize and accept the devic realms. While the landscaping of your garden might be traditional, the energy of it will reflect the degree to which you have tapped the light-heartedness and joy of the devas, the laughter of the nature spirits and the same qualities within yourself.

We are all at the beginning of something quite new. We don't know what kind of garden cooperative consciousness will produce, but we do know it is creating a beautiful garden here and in other places throughout the world. At Findhorn we feel there is so much yet to be done, and it is important that we are not the only ones involved in this exploration. Our work is just a guidepost to new realms of discovery, and we would appreciate hearing from others pioneering in this area. It will be from all of us exploring many possibilities that a new cooperative gardening practice will evolve.

There is a lot of talk about the "oneness of life," but what does this mean in my day to day experience?

Together with minerals, plants and animals, we make up the body and consciousness of a single living organism—Earth. We move within this body, intricately related to and dependent upon every other part of it. But as human beings with the power of self-reflection, we are unique within this system, for we stand back from it and look, listen, smell, taste and feel the beauty of this being, consciously. While the myriad forms and levels of it appear as separate, in even the most common experiences of our everyday lives, we affirm the interrelatedness of these forms. We breathe in the oxygen that plants contribute to the atmosphere; they breathe in the carbon dioxide we expel. The fruits and vegetables we eat bring the light of a single sun into our bodies.

What we call opposites are only complementary parts of a greater whole. Just as the darkness of night is as necessary to the cycle of life as is the creative energy of the sun, the emptiness or isolation we may experience one day serves to cleanse and open us to the lightness and joy of the next—if we

The Garden is one body.
As we feel the earth at Pineridge
So someone in the veg garden feels
the same body.

Awareness of our one body, where
each of us are.

APRIL 7 – 14. – SIGRID – in garden TUESDAY, THURSDAY
& SATURDAY

DT IS FORK
C. DT.

accept the natural process. This is not always easy, but we have many opportunities every day through which to learn of the unity in apparent separation. We can work toward it in every moment.

As we increasingly recognize the need to recreate balance in the environment of our planet, we are called upon to create a commensurate balance in our inner environment. Our physical bodies, our emotions, intellect and spirit all seek to contribute to the harmony and wholeness of our being. To deny one aspect for the sake of another is to create imbalance. To heal the Earth, which is our greater body, we must create an ecological balance within as well as without. We do so by recognizing that the basis of life is interrelationship.

Through love, we recognize and enhance the interrelationship of all life forms. As human beings, we can choose to see each element of creation as separate. Or we can choose to see the one life that is within them all. Love is the energy of acceptance that cuts through the apparent barriers and links us with every part of life. Loving and accepting every aspect of ourselves, we become whole. We begin to experience the compassion that allows us to feel and understand the essence of all forms of life. Through love we can blend with the consciousness of a plant or with the consciousness of another human being. We share the one limitless energy that is within all life forms and actions. When we accept and acknowledge the beauty and perfection of each form this energy takes, we experience oneness. As the devas have said, *You may call this energy positive and negative, even label it good and evil, but when the fruit of the Tree of Knowledge is digested, you will see that all things are one, having emerged from the wars of opposites to unity.*

What greater vision could be given humankind
than for God to say to us, "You are my beloveds.
Build with me, create with me."

FINDHORN: THE ORGANIC CENTER. The theme of the Findhorn garden—the cooperation of humanity with the kingdom of nature, as represented by the devas and the nature spirits—has great significance in reorienting our consciousness towards the more holistic and transmaterial outlook which planetary survival would seem to require of us. The importance of the garden, as indeed of all areas of the community, lies in demonstrating the processes of the organic nature of consciousness attuned to the center and oneness of all life. Such an attunement can invoke and use in balance the formative, creative energies of the universe for the transformation of matter and the rebuilding of the Earth.

At a time when much is being written about the possibilities of communication with extraterrestrial beings, it is instructive to realize that we are surrounded by a world of intelligent lives who wield the most potent forces on Earth and who are eagerly waiting to enter into renewing a meaningful dialogue with us. As Dorothy and Roc have eloquently pointed out in this book, these lives have much to teach us and, in turn, they look to humanity for help and instruction in furthering the causes of evolution. They offer us a true partnership, as well as affirming humanity's essential divinity. Humanity has been playing with the fringes of true power, and has come close to destroying its world in the process. Findhorn now demonstrates the entry into a shared realm of real power, consecrated by a partnership of love, wisdom and understanding.

Deeper than that lies another message, as well, which the cooperation demonstrated in the Findhorn garden and its community has to offer. Deva, elemental, human—all participate in and reflect the same universal processes of growth. Our planet is informed with a life and a spirit which is gradually unfolding itself, realizing its latent potentials. This process repeats itself on every level of being. It can be symbolized by the unfolding seed that reveals through the various life stages of a tree, a flower or a vegetable the wholeness of what it is. The esoteric traditions of all cultures speak of the "withinness" of things that seeks to externalize and to fulfill itself. If we think of our planet as an organic, growing system—a living being—then it, too, has an image of fulfillment buried within its seed center, an image that is using all of nature as its means of emergence.

Within such a concept, humanity occupies a unique position. We are the kingdom of synthesis: part of us has evolved from the Earth, part of us has descended from a higher and cosmic level. We are, the devas say, their brothers, once part of them, who diverged into a different course of evolution while still retaining devic qualities within our higher natures. We are linked to the elementals, as well. We share in the biosystem, the ecology, the psychic energies of the natural world of Earth, yet we participate in a world of thought and intuition and of spirit that extends beyond this world. Unlike the patterns that encompass the evolution of plants and animals, our evolution is open-ended, open to creative repatterning by our own consciousness. (This potential, which is basically spiritual, is dimly reflected in modern attempts at genetic engineering and bio-molecular manipulation to change hereditary programming.) We can become true Lords of Evolution, taking over our own development from the forces of planetary nature which have brought us this far and extending that awareness and ability to assist the entire field of Earth's evolution.

Thus, humanity represents the stage of Earth's unfoldment at which the planetary soul becomes not only self-aware but functionally and creatively conscious of the processes through which growth, awareness and the externalization of spirit through form take place. Such a consciousness can say not only, "I am," but it can also say, "I know *how* I am what I am. I know and can work with the processes of identity through which I am becoming what I am." The devas are personifications and embodiments of these processes. They represent to humanity the consciousness which it must manifest in order to take its next evolutionary step.

To me, the New Age consciousness is essentially self-aware and rooted in its organic center of identity, that point where consciousness emerges from pure being into dynamic becoming. Such a consciousness participates knowingly in the growth process by understanding that process and thus wielding its energies. The essence of all growth processes is, in fact, divinity. Therefore, this consciousness is aware of divinity, but not as a thing, a possession, nor as some external agency that directs it. Rather, divinity is the very core and source and identity of the process of its being. Living that process with awareness, the New Age consciousness is capable of becoming one with its "Father" or source. Revealing the secret of the creative power of organic, integrated growth is Findhorn's contribution to this unfolding consciousness within humanity.

The affirmation of the organic center of identity and the process of emergence pervades Findhorn. Whether perceived through the devic or elemental influences of the garden, through attunement to God and to divine guidance, or simply as the creative spirit working through individuals who are given freedom to fulfill themselves in relation to a creative community, this process is the true phenomenon of this center by the North Sea. They are not just growing vegetables and flowers on barren sand. They are working with the processes of emergence and drawing out of Earth its potential. This actualization of the living Self of the planet is what has transformed the barren sand into a garden. The same is true for the members of the community. These people are not unfolding because they are working in a garden, a pottery, a college, or any of the other activities in which Findhorn is now engaged. They are being transformed into new people because they are learning to identify with the process of themselves, rather than with their forms. They are learning to understand and to be the growth energies that are stored within the depths of their organic psyche, their seed center of individuality.

Findhorn sounds a note of return to nature, but this can be deceptive, for it is not just the nature of woodlands and forests, of meadowlands and gardens, of shaded glens and still lochs and ice-crowned peaks. The return is to the dynamics of nature, the "nature" of nature. It is a return to the soul and intelligence and divinity of nature of which humanity is an integral part and through which the spirit of man is revealed. This is the world that Findhorn demonstrates. This is the Findhorn garden story, the story of the processes by which the world was born and by which it evolves; the processes by which the world now reaches, with the help of humanity, for a new unity of spirit and release of energy in evolution.

In this demonstration, Findhorn and the garden straddle the past and the future. By drawing us back into myth and legend and into cooperation with the spirits of the Earth, the elves and fairies and gnomes, Findhorn invites us to a more ancient time when man was young and shared his world knowingly with these beings. This priceless gift of wonderment invites us to become as little children, dancing in an elven ring of quicksilver delight and walking near the majesty of the great god Pan. We are offered the renewal of links only recently forgotten in the rush to industrialize the Earth. Yet at the same time, Findhorn proclaims the image for humanity of a new maturity, the birth of the consciousness of participatory divinity, of co-creation with God.

On little more than three acres of land, one-half of a caravan park, these people are forelighting the destiny of the race, the Once and Future Race of the Garden, through consciously working to understand and to express the identity at the core of their organic center.

In this book you have read the story of these people and of Findhorn's remarkable garden. You have read of devas and nature spirits. Behind all of this, you are reading of yourself and the nature of the life you share. Whether you tend a garden or not, you are the gardener of your own being, the seed of your destiny. As demonstrated at Findhorn, the principles involved go far beyond gardening and embrace all activities of life. Perhaps in these pages you have discovered ways to make your own sandy places bloom with new life and to enter more fully into the cosmic adventure of living.